Animal Navigation

Animal Navigation

HOW ANIMALS FIND THEIR WAY ABOUT

J. D. CARTHY

M.A., PH.D.

CHARLES SCRIBNER'S SONS

NEW YORK

FIRST PUBLISHED IN 1956

PRINTED IN GREAT BRITAIN

To

MY WIFE

—for many reasons

ACKNOWLEDGMENTS

The author would like to thank Drs. C. G. Butler, J. S. Kennedy, H. W. Lissmann, F.R.S., and G. V. T. Matthews for their most helpful criticism but wishes to make it quite clear that none of the shortcomings of this book can be laid at their door.

He would also like to thank the following for permitting their photographs to be used to illustrate this book: frontispiece and plate 3, Dr. T. C. Schneirla; plate 1, Dr. D. P. Wilson; plates 4 and 5, J. G. M. Marquenie, Esq.; plate 6, Dr. William Beebe; plate 7, the Anti-locust Research Centre (Photo: Dr. D. L. Gunn); plate 8, Ornithological Research Institute, Vogelwarte Helgoland, Wilhelmshaven (photo: H. Rittinghaus); plate 9, Dr. G. V. T. Matthews; plate 10, R. M. Lockley, Esq.; plate 11, U.S. Fish and Wildlife Service (photo: Dr. George Kelez); plate 12, the Royal Society of London from Johs. Schmidt, 1923, *Phil. Trans. Roy. Soc. Lond., Ser. B.211*; plate 14, Dr. D. E. Sergeant.

Figure 25 is reprinted from Müller-Pouillet's *Lehrbuch der Physik* by permission of the publishers, Friedr. Vieweg und Sohn.

The quotation on page 136 is from the poem 'Cats' by A. S. J. Tessimond which appeared in *The Walls of Glass* and is quoted by kind permission of the author.

The news item on page 136 is quoted by permission of *The Times*.

SUGGESTED FURTHER READING

C. G. BUTLER	*The World of the Honeybee*
KARL VON FRISCH	*The Dancing Bees*
G. V. T. MATTHEWS	*Bird Navigation*
C. B. WILLIAMS	*Butterfly Migration*

CONTENTS

ILLUSTRATIONS

CHAPTER I

Animals and Men

⚓

W HEN men first ventured upon the sea in boats, they crept anxiously along the coasts, for their craft were simple and unsuited to the open sea. But even when ship-building improved and boats became seaworthy their crews still kept to the shore. Mediterranean trade was confined to coastwise routes for many hundreds of years, for the open waters were treacherous, with sudden storms and violent squalls. But in time the northern sailors set out upon the open sea and the Vikings reached North America at an early date.

Thereafter the history of human navigation is one of increasing accuracy in calculating position and finding direction with the aid of instruments. Though it is true that some people seem to have a highly developed sense of direction—so called—most navigators depend upon instruments to measure the position of the sun, its height above the horizon and so forth, for navigation by the sun is the only possible way on the open ocean. But for sun navigation accurate timekeeping is essential and the invention of a reliable chronometer permitted a great advance in the accuracy of position finding. A compass, made at first of magnetite, or lodestone, will give the direction in which a ship is sailing but without a way of determining position one cannot be certain how far a ship has sailed.

But, of course, men had to find their way over long distances before they took to the sea. Early man was probably a nomad who moved on to new ground when he had exhausted the old. On the land there are landmarks—hills, trees, rivers, etc. The old tracks in the south of England, the ley ways, can still be traced by the clumps of trees which marked them in open country and by the V-shaped nicks in the hills to which they headed. But on the sea there are no such features, only the sun by day and the stars by night to steer by, and since the sun moves, to use it for navigation is more complicated than following a fixed chain of features across the countryside.

Men set out from their homes by land or sea only if they believe there is something desirable at the end of the journey: riches, new lands or simply the possibility of adventure. Yet animals too set out on their travels for much the same reasons as we do, but in animal terms riches are new supplies of food, and new lands, better places for laying eggs and bringing up young. Nevertheless animals are not adventurous! The parallel is really rather imperfect, for human travellers are activated by a conscious desire to reach their goal while most animals are not even conscious of their needs, much less of how to fulfil them. The stream of Brighton-bound cars on an August Bank Holiday is not really equivalent to the trek of sandhoppers seawards from the dry to the moist sand where they are more likely to survive.

Animals need certain things from their environment apart from food. There are optimum conditions of temperature and humidity for example, and even of the mechanical structure of their surroundings. The hot, dry and hard surfaces of rocks, to take an extreme example, are inhospitable to animals, who cannot even burrow into them for shelter, as they can in the shifting sands of a desert. Though animals appear to choose their habitats, vacating others to move to them, in reality it is innate behaviour, not conscious choice, that impels them. Those which prefer moisture may be restless on dry surfaces, but become quiescent in wet places. Others shun the light which drives them into the cool, moist, dark places they prefer.

The world of an animal is, then, a patchwork of places where the living conditions are bad, not so bad and good. For various reasons the pattern changes frequently; moist soils dry up, leaves die and no longer give shelter from the sun, and a hundred and one accidents of nature, as well as the changes of the seasons, will influence it, and the animals must move away. Sometimes the distance they must travel is measured in millimetres, sometimes in hundreds of miles. A protozoan need swim only a tiny distance to avoid a local concentration of carbon dioxide in the water, while birds migrate across continents to favourable breeding places, but even the protozoan's journey, short as it is by our measure, is long for a creature of its small size.

How to get to the new place presents a problem. The bigger animals like birds and even some insects actually seem to aim for a definite point. The annual visits of swifts and swallows to the same localities, and often to the same nests, are witness to the accuracy with which birds navigate. And the bees, laden with honey or pollen, that cluster round the hive entrance, have returned from flowers hundreds of yards away; they use methods of navigation which are like some we ourselves use—though no animal carries a compass or uses anything comparable with the electronic devices upon which modern travel is becoming increasingly dependent.

The sun is the main beacon, not surprisingly as it is absolutely certain to be in the sky by day. But animals may be able to perceive aspects of the sun's presence which we cannot. Though some animals are sensitive, few people can see in the sky the pattern of polarized light which is intimately connected with the source of light which forms it, the sun itself. But, bee or bird, they also learn to recognize landmarks, selecting them to mark the route or to pinpoint places where they must alter course, just as the ancient navigators watched the shape of the shoreline for familiar towers and hills. By this means an area becomes familiar and the animal can return to its nest or its colony from anywhere within it. More remarkable still is the ability to return home from unfamiliar places where the landmarks are unknown, which demands from birds and some mammals an ability to judge their position in relation to their home— whether (to use human terms) they are to the east or west, north or south of it, thereby determining the direction in which they must move.

The insect's world is a world of scent, as well as colour, light and shape. We have only a poor idea of the splendour of this olfactory universe, like colour-blind men gazing at a painting full of subtle nuances of colour. But a track can be marked by the scents which linger round it as well as by the trees and grasses which surround it. To this we are insensitive, but dogs and insects are acutely perceptive of odours and tastes.

Navigation seems to imply guidance to a goal, though the more intrepid explorers were those who sailed into the unknown, ignorant of, or perhaps preferring not to know, what awaited them. They are none the less granted the name of Navigators. Many animals, particularly the smaller invertebrates, make their ways about in an erratic search for suitable dwelling places. They do not know, in the human sense, what their goal is, nor where they are liable to find those near-ideal conditions which they seek. They wander on, encountering the right places by chance, but the probability of their finding the most favourable is increased by their inborn reactions to certain kinds of stimuli. When they encounter weak stimuli of the right sort they seek the source, which will be an area of stronger favourable stimulation. Thus an animal searching for food will creep up the gradient of chemical concentration from the weak outer fringes to the stronger centre where the food will be.

Some of the goal-less animals twist and turn in their search, but others go long distances along straight paths. It seems probable that this is the more efficient way of searching, though, since we know little, if anything, about the detailed distribution of favoured places for one of these small animals it would be hard to prove. However that may be, these animals—and most of the ones we know about are insects—do keep on their straight course by navigation. We know they do this because if we change their surroundings they react in the way we would expect. Thus, if we shade the sun from an ant and arrange a mirror so that the sun's rays now come from the opposite side, the ant turns round and runs in the opposite direction. Or again, the caterpillars of the pine sawfly crawl along in a straight line but turning a polarized light filter held over them may cause them to alter direction by turning through the same angle. In both cases the insects were navigating and were dependent upon these two stimuli for their direction.

We shall see that in both long- and short-distance navigation the same sorts of beacons are used, but the ways in which animals use them may not be ours.

CHAPTER II

Scent Trails

T HE fog comes down into our city streets and we fumble our way home. Our familiar landmarks are gone and we must depend upon groping hands and a timidly extended foot. But even in our partial blindness one sort of landmark suddenly obtrudes itself into our thoughts, as the smell of the fish-and-chip shop on the corner grows stronger, until we know for certain where we are. Man's sense of smell is not well developed; it is, in fact, so poor that when we watch a dog snuffling along a street or a country lane we cannot imagine the rich world of smell in which he lives. Many other animals besides dogs use their sense of smell, for man and birds are the exception to the general rule of well-developed sensitivity to chemical substances. Many mammals mark their territory with scent. Food and mates are recognized and located by their scents in many creatures as will be shown by the extraordinary journeys made by male moths in search of females, which we shall discuss later (Chapter X).

A good example, and a familiar one to zoologists, is the way in which planarians find their food. Planarians are small, flat worms, with simple internal organization. Their mouth opens at the end of a proboscis normally concealed in a pocket half-way along the body. They are carnivorous and some live in streams. These worms crawl along the bottom moving in straight lines until they come near food, from which juices containing attractive chemicals are diffusing into the surrounding water. On the worm's head are organs sensitive to these chemicals, and, as soon as they are stimulated, the worm begins to make side-to-side movements with its head. It tests the water on either side of its path: as it

1 A Whelk, its siphon is protruded from its shell above its tentacles

2 Section of an ant's trail. The longer streaks are two to three millimetres long. The trail has been dusted with lycopodium powder which sticks on to the streaks

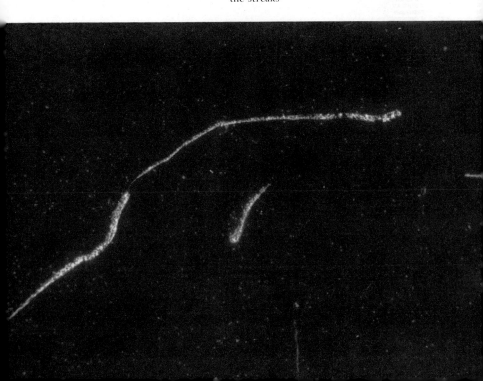

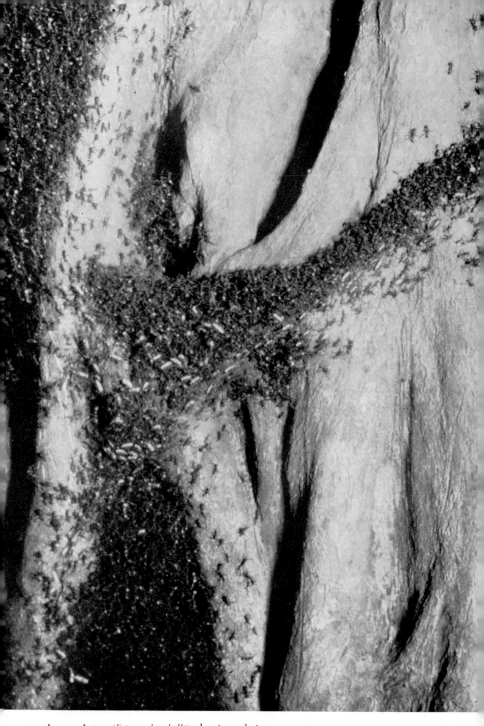

3 Army Ants (*Eciton burchelli*) leaving their
bivouac (at left) bearing with them nearly mature
worker larvæ

turns towards the food it encounters greater chemical stimulation than when it turns away (fig. 1). So, always swerving to the side which is most stimulated, it moves in a long curve towards the

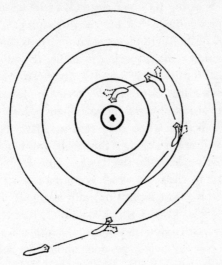

Fig. 1.—A planarian reaches food by testing the water and turning towards the greater chemical stimulation. The rings represent the diffusion outwards of food chemicals.

food until finally it is close enough to put out its proboscis and start feeding.

This is a perfectly simple but an extremely effective device. Though it is automatic, in that the worm does not 'think,' it is not completely invariable, for only a hungry worm is drawn to the food; after it is satiated, food chemicals lose their stimulating power—a useful economy in behaviour, which is found in many animals. When a particular physiological need is satisfied, then the behaviour that has resulted in that satisfaction is temporarily abolished, coming again into full play when the need arises.

This kind of behaviour—comparing the amount of chemical in two different places successively, as opposed to comparing them at the same time—is fairly common among invertebrate animals. Probably whelks, crawling on the sea floor (plate 1), find their food in a similar way, testing the surroundings by sucking water in through their siphons from different places, moving their siphons round instead of their heads. When the flat worm moves its head it is bringing its sense organs in contact with different parts of its surroundings, but the moving siphon of the mollusc brings samples of the surrounding sea-water into contact with the sense organ which remains stationary inside the animal.

But chemical sensitivity is raised to its greatest importance in the social insects. Bees, for example, recognize flowers that other workers have visited by the flower scent which the foragers carry on their bodies when they return. After flying out they confirm that they are at the right flowers by another scent that the foragers themselves leave on the flowers. Ants and bees recognize their nest mates by the scent which is common to all the insects in the nest. But this is not navigation, only recognition.

It is in the social insects which are blind, that is, all termites and some ants, that odour becomes all important. Deprived of sight they become entirely dependent upon scent and touch. The workers in their search for food follow trails from their nests to their foraging places, recognizing them by their smell, though their sense of smell is not like ours but is more akin to our taste. Though ants can smell odours—that is, air-borne chemical substances—they can also sense chemicals by touch, in just the same way that we taste salty things when they touch the sensitive cells on our tongues. But this sense resides in the ant's antennæ and not in their mouths. When they touch an object with their antennæ they in effect 'taste' it. You can watch them tapping food with their antennæ, moving the tips of the feelers lightly to and fro over the surface. All ants have this power well developed, even if they can see, for they must make use of chemical guides in the darkness of the nest; they sense the nest odour of an intruder, recognizing her as a friend or foe.

Not all ants leave the nest to search for food, in fact the number of foragers may be a very small proportion of the thousands of insects in the nest. It is the same with honey-bees and termites. The ones that stay behind have to be fed with the food brought back by the travellers, and there are all the hundreds of larvæ to be fed, too, the voracious, quickly-growing young which will change into more workers to replace those that die. The life of the colony depends upon the safe return of the foragers bearing food, so it is not surprising that in social insects, using the landmarks they see and the landmarks they smell, methods of navigation are well developed.

It was the eighteenth-century French biologist, Bonnet, who first recorded his observations on the trails of ants, though no doubt many little boys and grown men had earlier played at interrupting the traffic along these paths. Bonnet found a colony of ants established in the head of a teazle and brought it indoors. He placed it at one end of a table and at the other end placed a pile of sugar; he then watched ants coming down the stem across the table to the pile, picking up sugar and scurrying back with it. They ran to and fro along a straight track, none of them wandering far from it. He wondered why they kept to such a definite path. It did not seem to be a matter of walking to or from the light, so he sought to find what it was that held them to their narrow way. He rubbed his finger across the path in front of an ant running towards the sugar. The ant stopped and searched about when it reached the place, waving its antennæ in the air at one moment and tapping the ground around itself the next. There was a gradual crowding of foragers on both sides of the line, some coming from the nest, some from the food. These ants ran back and forth until one or two, more adventurous perhaps than the rest, ran on to the place where he had rubbed his finger. Foragers from both sides met, recognized each other and continued on their interrupted journey. Gradually the trail was re-established, for a trail it seemed to be that he had destroyed with his finger and almost certainly a trail of chemicals which the ants could smell.

But it was not until the end of the nineteenth century that the seat of this sense was located. The great Swiss entomologist, Auguste Forel, found various organs on an ant's antennæ which seemed by their structure to be particularly well adapted for reacting to chemical substances. Some are flat, some like short stubby hairs, but all supplied by nerves (fig. 2). Other insects have similar organs and they are usually situated on the antennæ in very large numbers, though they may also appear on the feet or on the

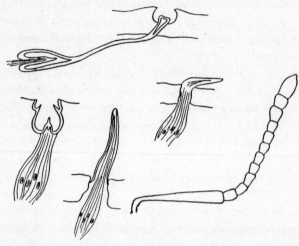

FIG. 2.—Various forms of chemo-sensitive hairs which may be found on the antennæ of an ant, such as that shown on the right. At the base of each hair is a bunch of sensory cells. (After Wheeler.)

mouth palps. Not only did Forel consider that these organs sensed the smell of things they touched, but that the ants could also perceive the shape of an odour! This is impossible for us to imagine, for we have undeveloped, or at most poorly developed olfactory imagination; our imaginings spring mainly from what we see and hear. We see a patch of light of a certain wavelength and we call it red; this is a sensation just as a particular smell is a sensation. Now if that patch is in the shape of an arrow, we see red and arrow shape. An ant smells a smell as being of a certain shape, so that if a smear of a smelly substance is wider at one end than the other it can tell which end is wider. It is as if we could recognize a bullseye sweet not by its black stripes but by its pepperminty roundness. Forel's suggestion, which may not be entirely acceptable, arose from watching the movements of ants' antennæ, twitching about like callipers estimating shapes. Indeed they are so mobile and independent of each other that it was reasonable to assume that they can follow outlines.

Foragers with their abdomens full of food always make their

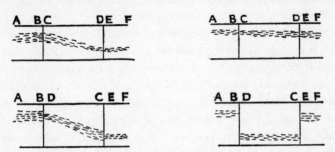

FIG. 3.—Diagram to show the effect of reversal of a segment of a trail laid by ants. Note that in the right-hand example, the continuity of the trail is disturbed by reversing the segment.

way back to the nest unless they are disturbed. And foragers leaving the nest always follow the trail towards the food. Can it be that ants know at which end of the trail the food is and at which the nest? Forel believed that they did, for he thought that they could tell the difference between the right and left sides of the track, which, he said, must be differently shaped unless the sides of the track are exactly parallel, which is most unlikely.

There seemed to be some evidence that the trail was organized into a nestwards and a foodwards direction. Ants were made to run over a row of pieces of card until the card had become soaked with odour, forming a trail. When the pieces were transposed (fig. 3) the ants were not confused, but if any of them were reversed the ants were disturbed and halted when they got to either end of the reversed section. It looked as if there was a right and a wrong way round. But how could the trails be polarized? Were they built up of the footprints of the workers which scurried back and forth along them? Each footprint, like a human one, might have a 'heel and toe,' so that some would be pointing towards the food and others to the nest. But since almost every forager does return to the nest, the number of footprints facing

21

each way would be about the same. Perhaps the footprints of the home-going ants might differ because the workers are laden with food, so that ants could distinguish them from those of the outgoing unladen foragers. Yet this is impossible, for an ant's feet, all six of them, do not point in one direction as it runs, and anyway the trail is laid down by hundreds of foragers running all over it, there is no rule of the road and the tracks are inextricably mixed.

Another suggestion was that there might be a gradient of food odour, strongest, naturally, at the food end of the trail, dwindling nestwards with, conversely, a gradient of nest odour outwards from the nest. These odours would occur because an ant while in the nest would be covered with nest smell, which would diminish as it moved towards the food. But again if this happened in individual trails the ant could not find its way from the tangled skein of tracks.

These theories arose from the observation that ants were upset when a section of their trail was reversed, but we can suppose another explanation for their disturbance. Rearrangement of sections of the track without reversing them can sometimes stop the stream of ants, especially if the ends of the trails on the transposed pieces do not coincide. The trail is broken by this change round as it may also be by reversing a section (fig. 3). This explanation eliminates the idea of trail polarization, which is rather difficult to accept and even more difficult to explain satisfactorily.

When trail-laying ants are on the move—and not all species do lay trails—they stop occasionally and extend their legs, tuck their abdomens in under the rest of their bodies, and stroke the ground with the tip of the abdomen. You can see the British jet black ant do this, and North African ants have been described as performing the same movements; no doubt many others do as well. If the ants walk on glass, you find a tiny drop of material on the glass which has been left by the ant's abdomen. It is drawn out in the direction in which the ant is going (plate 2), just like toothpaste which has been squeezed from the tube, touched on the ground and pulled along until all of it has been dragged off. This trail spot is squeezed out of a tube, too, the tube of the ant's intestine. So each mark has a shape and points in the direction the ant is running, but there is no evidence that the ants perceive this. When they follow a trail they do not feel round each spot as if sensing its shape, but one antenna taps the trail occasionally, keeping literally 'in touch' with it but no more. The marks are all mixed up and it is difficult to follow any one series.

Now let us try wiping out the trail. We draw a finger across the path in front of a forager. She reaches the point and then advances no farther but dashes back and forth with antennæ waving violently. Then gradually, but only gradually, the trail is restored. Yet if we wipe out the trail with a piece of cotton wool and not a finger, the ants cross a gap of an inch without hesitation! So interruption of the trail does not upset the ant, it seems to be carried on by its momentum for at least a short distance. The fact that a finger-smear causes confusion suggests that we leave some substance behind which is strange to the ant, an unexpected odour which it encounters among the others along the trail that have become familiar to it. That, and not the break in the trail, is surely what causes the confusion.

Not all the ants we watch lay trails. It seems as if only those which are successful in finding food leave the smears as they run back to the nest. Success seems also to engender excitement in an ant, just as in man—an infectious excitement, for once back in the nest, the other workers are stirred by the tapping antennæ of the forager and accept food from her. They are wakened from their comparative lethargy to dash about in the nest and to run out from it. When they emerge they encounter the trail which has been laid, and follow it. Since they start from the nest end they go foodwards. If the food supply is still abundant they take their fill and run back, reinforcing the trail with more smears. Thus, only if the trail leads to food will it be preserved and kept fresh. When the food supply dwindles, the excitement of the foragers decreases, the trail goes unstrengthened, its vigour fades and foragers coming out of the nest are no longer drawn along it but follow some new path to some new supply. This means that the foraging potential of the colony will be used economically and no effort will be wasted on places from which the food has gone.

This means, of course, that the scent marks do not retain their attractiveness for more than a matter of minutes, or an hour or two at the most, otherwise any number of trails would be drawing foragers along them. But the chemicals marking the trail of the army ants of Central America seem to last much longer, even as long as thirty-one days in the dry season. These ants are totally blind and in order to keep together depend upon touching, 'tasting' and smelling their companions. We know a great deal about their social organization from the work of Dr. T. C. Schneirla of the American Museum of Natural History. Their life is nomadic. They do not make permanent nests, but spend days wandering in a long column, halting each night. At these bivouacs the whole colony forms the nest, suspended, walled in by a living mat of ants (plate 3). From this bivouac raiding columns go out into the surrounding country and then finally the whole colony follows one of these raiding columns to a new temporary bivouac. Every so often, however, they halt for a longer period and then the colony hangs in some shelter, some species even seeking a hole in the ground. This is the period when the larvæ have pupated and a new batch of eggs is laid. All is still in the colony by comparison with the urgent stirrings of the larvæ when the colony is wandering; and even raiding and food collecting are reduced. Then larvæ hatch from the eggs and adults begin to move in the pupal cases, the colony reawakens and the daily marches recommence.

The blind workers hurry out in the raiding columns, encountering other workers pushing their way back to the colony. Workers which get to the edge of the column seem to be turned back by the absence of the smell of familiar chemicals and the absence of contact with other ants. At the tip of the column advancing over the jungle floor, and capturing any booty it can find, new territory is being soaked with chemical substances as the leading ants advance a short distance and then retreat again into the column. The front of the column rolls forward like a wave up a beach. But the columns are kept close packed (frontispiece) so that no workers stray, each being guided by the chemicals laid by its nest companions, and even sometimes by other species, for a column may follow an old trail which may be one of its own or one left by another species. In the dry season the jungle becomes a network of these tracks, and Schneirla has suggested that the males which fly from the nest land on these trails and by following them are led to the colonies, making use of the foraging paths of the workers.

These paths do not seem to be of orientated smell spots and as we have seen there is not yet conclusive evidence that ant trails are directional. But there are times when something of this sort seems to happen. Macgregor watched some red ants foraging in the laboratory and he noticed that they found their way back to the nest only if they passed over a particular place; at least, the paths of all the ants which returned fairly directly crossed this point, after which they went straight to the nest entrance (fig. 4). But if an ant missed this spot, then she wandered about quite widely before finding the nest entrance apparently by chance. This spot seemed to act as a signpost. Moreover, he found that blind ants were able to use this guide sign, which suggests the spot had a shaped smell, an odour arrow pointing to the nest entrance. At least on this occasion the workers were using their contact-odour sense to guide them.

It is not really surprising that such apparently contradictory results should emerge from experiments. Because route-finding is so important to social insects, it is unlikely that it would depend upon one sense alone; it is much more likely that a safe return is ensured by learning the route in terms of several senses. This is particularly necessary to insects that run on the ground, for there will be times when among the grasses the sky will be obscured and distant landmarks hidden; temporarily blinded the ant must turn to some other sense, such as its sensitivity to chemicals. An insect which flies does not have its beacons obscured so easily during its flight and does not need this double assurance, even if it were possible. Under the controlled unnatural conditions of the laboratory one may at one time evoke one sort of orientation, at another a different one without the results really being in conflict.

It is a far cry from fish and chips to the odour trails of ants in

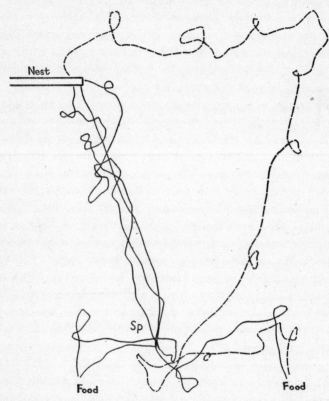

Fig. 4.—The tracks of ants returning to the nest, reached through the tube. Those that pass over the guiding spot (Sp) reach the nest entrance more directly than those which fail to run over it. (After Macgregor.)

Central America, but if we had the sensitivity of ants to smells, and most particularly their contact odour sense, we might 'olfactorize' the world around us in the thickest fog just as we visualize it now as our groping fingers touch brickwork and shop-front.

CHAPTER III

Home is the Hunter

✴

MANY wasps, near relatives of ants, live solitary lives. Unlike the familiar wasps of the summer tea-table which live in nests containing thousands of insects, each of these solitary wasps digs small burrows for its young. At the ends of these short tunnels it lays its eggs, often a single one in each burrow, and with the eggs is put some food for the larvæ when they hatch. This food consists of paralysed insects or spiders captured by the female wasps, some of which store away enough to last the larva until it pupates before emerging as an adult, while others leave only a little, returning at intervals after the larvæ are hatched to supply them with more.

Now these nests are tiny and the entrances are not at all obvious. Often the wasps close their nests after leaving them and it is clear that they are not easy to find. Yet a wasp flying out to capture a caterpillar or a spider hundreds of yards away must be able to return to the nest or all its efforts in finding and seizing the food will have been in vain. In fact some of the wasps found in the hotter countries catch their prey before they make a hole, but usually their prey is so big that one insect is enough to supply the needs of the larva. Generally it is as important for them to find their way as it is for ant foragers to carry their loads of food back to the hungry workers and larvæ in the nest. If it has already packed away some food in the nest all those supplies will be wasted if the wasp cannot push in the last body and lay an egg on the heap of supplies. On the other hand wasps which provide the egg with all its food leave the nest alone after the egg is laid and apparently never return. Those that continue to feed the larva leave it alone only when it has finished feeding and has turned into a pupa. The wasp need only remember the nest for a short time when it stores all the food at once, perhaps for eight or ten journeys, and all performed in a day, before it starts to provision a new hole. But if it is to return at intervals to feed its growing larva, its memory must be longer.

It has been known for many years that these wasps are disturbed and unable to find their nests when a large stone or branch lying in the vicinity is moved away. Instead of landing beside the nest hole and crawling quickly inside, the wasp circles about sometimes fluttering its wings as it searches for the entrance. This is quite a different sight from an undisturbed wasp's direct and speedy return. Watching these insects has a certain fascination as many have discovered to their cost as they sit entranced, losing all sense of time, missing lunch, tea and even supper, if darkness does not fall to break the spell. One can sympathize with the French entomologist, who, having disturbed the surroundings of one such wasp's nest, awaited the return of the insect to see what happened, consulted his watch, considering his hostess's feelings if he were late for what he knew would be a fine meal, and finally cast all aside to continue his vigil. It is plain from the confusion of the wasp that it has learnt the landmarks near its nest and depends upon them being in their usual place.

But the true wonder of the wasp's choice of landmarks did not emerge until a group of Dutch entomologists proceeded to test and trick one kind of wasp in an endeavour to find out just what it could see. If we are not careful we are inclined to think that any animal can see the world around it in the way we do, but we forget that some see no colours and that to some their surroundings are flat as if painted on a canvas with little or no indication of depth and distance. We can test an animal's power of perception by seeing whether it can distinguish between two models which differ in one characteristic, say, colour, or size, or shape. By taking the characteristics of objects in the surroundings one by one we can build up some sort of a picture of the animal's visual world.

The Dutch zoologist Tinbergen and his helpers worked in this way when they studied the homing of the bee-wolf, *Philanthus triangulum*, on the sandy heaths of central Holland. Here on bare sandy patches the female wasps dig their nests, kicking the sand backwards between their hind legs like a dog digging out a rat

Fig. 5.—A ring of fircones is arranged about a foot away from the sandfleck round a bee-wolf's nest to test whether it returns to the nest or to the cones.

hole. The sand falls behind them forming a 'fleck'; sometimes this appears as a light patch as the wasp comes to the lighter sand below the darker upper layers (fig. 5). Soon, its nest completed, the wasp flies off to look for its prey, searching out a bee which it captures and paralyses before flying back to the hole. It lands close to the hole (plate 5) and drags the bee inside, emerging a little later to fly off to find another.

Now just what is there about the nest and its surroundings which the wasp can remember and recognize when it returns? There is the usual debris scattered around on the sandy earth, twigs, fir cones and so on, as well as small bushes and clumps of heather. These might serve. But we can do more than guess what the wasp sees. If we arrange fir cones in a ring round the nest hole before the wasp flies away, then when it has gone move them aside so that the real hole and its sand fleck are no longer surrounded, we can see what the wasp does when it comes back. It flies towards the ring, and alights in the middle of it, ignoring the real position of its nest (fig. 5). If we scare it away it flies back again to the ring after we stop waving our hands at it. It lands and scurries about on the ground searching for the hole which is not there. Again we scare it off and again it returns. So it

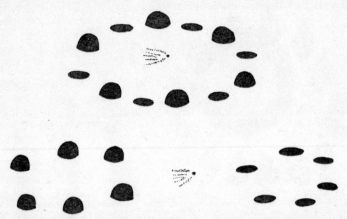

FIG. 6.—The arrangement of black discs and hemispheres around the nest of a bee-wolf before testing whether it can distinguish between flat objects and tall ones. The arrangement when testing the wasp is shown below.

goes on until quite by accident it finds its real nest which it is bound to do unless the ring is a very great distance from it. So now we know that the wasp has noticed the cones surrounding its nest and guided its return flight by them.

Some landmarks are probably more obvious to a wasp than others and these are the ones which are memorized. We tend also to choose the more obvious landmarks when we are memorizing a route and we choose those features whose character- istics are more familiar and more to our liking. Some of us tend to remember our way by remembering the public houses we pass, others of us the churches. So also does the wasp recognize certain things in its surroundings because their attributes are those which appear most obvious to it. Suppose, for instance, that the ring of fir cones is replaced by a ring of eight flat black discs and eight black hemispheres of the same radius as the discs; let them be arranged so that we have disc—hemisphere—disc— hemisphere and so on (fig. 6). Then when the wasp is away hunting, move the eight discs to one side of the nest and arrange them in a ring, and the eight hemispheres to the other side and put them down in a ring too (fig. 6). There are several possibilities of what may happen when the wasp comes back and sees the two

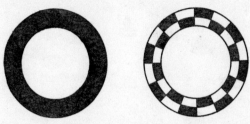

FIG. 7.—Types of plain black and chequered rings used in the experiments. (After Tinbergen.)

patterns. It may not be able to distinguish between flat discs and the hemispheres, and will then fly to one or other of the two rings choosing both of them equally often. Or it may concentrate on the discs or the hemispheres, ignoring the other ring. And this is what happens, for the wasp visits the hemispheres more frequently than the discs; on one occasion, for example, making eighteen visits as against none to the circle of discs. Now both objects had the same surface area and both were black, the only difference being that the discs were flat and the hemispheres solid. So it looks very much as if the wasp prefers solidity to flatness.

The wasp prefers the object which it selects as landmark to have a well-broken outline, and when offered the choice between a plain black ring and a black and white chequered ring, it selects the latter (fig. 7). Like the honey-bees it prefers the smaller checks to the larger ones (fig. 20), for the more subdivisions the more broken is the pattern.

It is not surprising to find also that the wasps prefer objects standing on the ground to those sunk into it. Tinbergen showed this most neatly by making a number of hollow black cones, all of the same size. Then he arranged sixteen of them around the nest, alternately pushing them point downwards into the sand or standing them point upwards (fig. 8). When the returning wasp was faced with the choice of a ring of black cones point upwards, or a ring of buried cones with only their bases showing at the surface, it chose the ones which stood out from the soil.

Fig. 8.—An arrangement of twelve cones around a wasp's nest.

Now this might have been due to preference for shadows, for only the standing cones would cast a shadow, but later experiments disproved this. Some black shapes were made of flat cardboard so that when they were pushed into the ground on edge, only a half-circle of black stood up above the soil. First a wasp was trained to go to a ring of hemispheres, then it was tested by offering it a ring of the flat black shapes arranged in either of the ways shown in fig. 9 as an alternative to the hemispheres. When the shapes were arranged to radiate from the nest the wasp continued to visit the hemispheres; however, when they were arranged in a circle around the nest, the wasp preferred this ring slightly more than the hemispheres. Clearly as these presented silhouettes similar to those of the hemispheres when viewed from the centre of the ring the wasp was confused in its choice and could no longer distinguish the two rings apart with any certainty. Since the shadows cast by both of the arrangements of flat shapes was the same, shadow seems to have little importance.

This provides a clue to the moment at which the wasp makes its reconnaissance of its surroundings. We know that on leaving its nest hole for the first time after a new set of objects have been put round it, the wasp circles for a minute or two before flying

4 A bee-wolf wasp (*Philanthus triangulum*) holding her prey, a honey-bee, while digging out the closed entrance of her nest

5 A solitary wasp (*Bembex rostrata*) grasping a fly, about to land on her nest (in the lower right hand corner of the photograph)

6 Moths deflected to lights while migrating through Portachuelo Pass

off. It seems very likely, as we shall see later, that it is then learning the position of its nest in relation to more distant landmarks. However, the moment when the flat plates appear

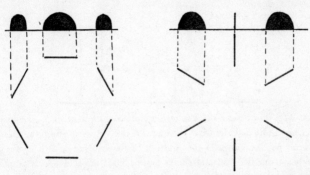

FIG. 9.—The two arrangements of flat black shapes used in the experiments (see text) in plan and elevation. (After Tinbergen and Kruyt.)

most like hemispheres would be when the wasp looks at them from ground level inside the circle, not from the air above it.

There is another piece of evidence which supports this idea that the wasp learns its immediate surroundings while it is still on the ground. Blocks of wood placed near the nest are more attractive than ones of the same size placed twice as far away. If, however, instead of putting blocks of the same size at that distance we put blocks which are twice as high as those near the nest, then the wasp does not show any particular preference for either the near ones or the more distant taller ones. The tops of both of these sets of cubes will be at the same angle to the nest hole (fig. 10), or, in other words, they will look equally tall to an insect emerging from the hole, though when the nearer and the more distant cubes are of the same height, the nearer ones will look tallest from that position and in fact they are preferred for that reason. It appears, then, very much as if the wasp makes its choice of the different objects close to the nest just as it comes out from below the ground.

The landmarks chosen are tall and preferably have a broken outline. Although the wasp apparently notes them from the

C   33

ground, it sees them from the air when it returns, for it hovers two or three metres above the landmarks before descending to them slowly. It is of interest that another solitary wasp, *Bembex*

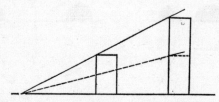

FIG. 10.—To show that a cube subtends the same angle at the nest entrance as another cube half its size placed half the distance from the nest. The dotted outline indicates the position of the smaller cube if it was placed farther from the nest and shows the reduced angle which it would then subtend.

rostrata, also learns its landmarks from ground level, in fact, at the time it is digging its nest (plate 5). But this wasp, which flies faster and lower than the bee-wolf, is less influenced by height than by objects with a large surface area.

Yet a bee-wolf's choice does not fall entirely upon particular objects but also on particular patterns of arrangement. For a wasp whose nest is surrounded by a ring of fir cones will still return there without hesitation if the cones are replaced by pieces of black wood and will ignore the fir cones piled close by. It is returning to a nest surrounded by a ring and it does not matter of what that ring consists. In fact the bee-wolf will pick out a ring shape from a bigger pattern, as it did in the experiments when it always flew to the centre of the 'pan' of the 'Dipper' when fir cones were put out in the shape shown in fig. 11.

But to find the way back it is not enough to memorize the nest-hole and its immediate surroundings. That group of objects might be anywhere and the wasp must know where they are with respect to bigger and more distant landmarks, just as we too find our way first by big landmarks until we reach the neighbourhood we are seeking, and then look for less conspicuous landmarks close to our goal. So also does the wasp learn the relative positions of nest and distant objects during her orientation flight which only lasts for from 30 to 100 seconds.

One of the Dutch biologists, van Beusekom, put a flat square of

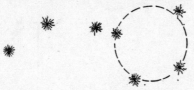

FIG. 11.—Diagram of the arrangement of fir cones in the shape of the Great Bear. The dotted circle shows the cones which are apparently seen as a circle by a wasp.

wood down by one of the nest holes so that one corner pointed at the hole. On the other side of the hole, but some distance away, he pushed a branch into the ground (fig. 12). When the wasp had learned the position of its nest it searched only around that corner of the square which pointed at the branch, and, of course, at the hole. Then, while it was away foraging van Beusekom turned the square through 45 deg. so that one *side* now lay towards the nest. The wasp returned and was clearly confused, for it searched at two of the corners of the square, the two which lay on the side of the square towards the branch. If the branch was moved either to left or right, the wasp's attention was transferred to either the left corner or the right one (fig. 12). So it was plain that it was not only a corner which was the landmark but one corner in particular—the corner nearest the branch. In the same way that the wasp appreciated the ring of cones as a ring not as a mere collection of cones, so the pattern corner-hole-bush was what the wasp learned here.

As this wasp leaves its hole, then, it memorizes the objects close to the nest, and during its orientation flight it learns their relationship to other objects before it flies off to the hunting grounds. Unless an experimenter alters the surroundings, or there is a period of bad weather which keeps the wasp below ground, one orientation flight suffices and after that the outward-bound wasp flies straight off without hesitation.

This goes some way then to explaining how the bee-wolf finds its way back, but there are other wasps which sometimes pick on such large prey that they cannot fly back with it but have to drag

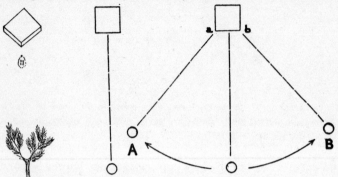

Fig. 12.—Left, the arrangement of wooden square and branch (see text). Centre, the square is turned so that its side faces the nest; either of its nearer corners are now visited by the wasp. Right, when the branch is moved to one side the wasp visits the appropriate corner. (After van Beusekom.)

it along the ground. This seems to present another problem because the wasp has flown out but has to walk back: apparently it learns its landmarks from an aerial viewpoint, but sees and recognizes them as it returns from ground-level—a remarkable ability, akin to that of the more intelligent vertebrates to recognize a shape (say, a letter A) of any size from any angle. Even though the patterns of light which fall on the retina of the eye will vary, yet they are in each case recognized as the same thing.

One of the wasps that drags its prey back to the nest is *Ammophila campestris*, the heath sand-wasp, which chooses caterpillars as food for its larvæ. Sometimes these caterpillars are too large to be carried in flight. The wasp therefore picks it up in its jaws, grasping it behind the head, and carries it along slung between its legs, after immobilizing it by stinging it. And the problem of finding the nest is made doubly difficult because each time the wasp leaves, it closes the entrance so that there is little sign of it at a casual glance.

Trees are the main landmarks for this insect. When a row of

artificial 'trees' was put up to lead to its nest and the wasp was released at the other end of the row it flew along the line and found its nest at the end. The row was then displaced sideways

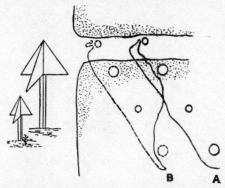

FIG. 13.—An imitation tree (left). The solid circles on the right show the position of the trees originally and the broken circles after they were moved. The tracks of the wasp from **A** and **B** when the trees were in their original positions are shown by the continuous line and that from B, after the trees were moved, by the broken line. (After Baerends.)

and the wasp was again released at the end. This time it followed the row as before but of course it no longer led to the nest (fig. 13), and it searched at the end of the row in vain. The 'trees' were later put back in their original places and the wasp was recaptured. This time it was released at the place where the row had last been, it flew immediately to the 'trees' and followed them to its nest. Plainly it had learned that the 'trees' led to the nest and it used them as markers for its path.

Now this wasp flies differently from the bee-wolf, for it 'hedge-hops' as it searches for its prey, flying at the level of the tops of the heath clumps. On its return journey, if it is walking back, it frequently climbs to the tops of the heather clumps—to the same level as its outward flight, in other words—apparently takes a sight on a landmark, descends, picks up the caterpillar again and sets off. The most useful beacon under these conditions would be something large enough to be seen from the ground, hence the wasp's preference for trees.

Another remarkable thing about this wasp is that it may concern itself with three or four nests at once, all of them at different stages of construction or of stocking with food. As each

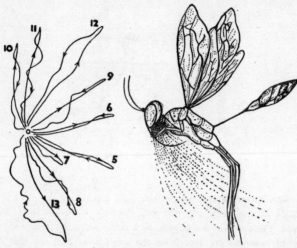

FIG. 14.—Right, a sand-wasp distributing sand which it has dug out. On left, the tracks of its successive outward and return flights while digging. (After Baerends.)

one is fully provisioned and the egg is laid, the wasp closes the nest and leaves it. But it soon starts to dig another, so there are always several on hand at once.

This wasp rarely circles above its nest as it leaves it, for its memory of the location seems to be long-lasting. Probably the surroundings are memorized as the nest is being built. The method of digging the hole is to take mouthfuls of sand and fly away scattering them and then return for another mouthful (fig. 14). When doing this it flies straight out from the nest, at first returning along the same track. After several journeys in various directions, the wasp begins, however, to wander on its return and not to follow its outward route so slavishly. This suggests that it is becoming more familiar with the surroundings and so can afford to stray (fig. 14). If this is so it would explain why orientation flights are so rarely observed except after particularly bad weather has altered the appearance of the nest surroundings.

Quite a considerable area around the nest is known to this wasp, for if it is carried away from the temporary home that it is visiting, it will return there fairly quickly. But the further it is

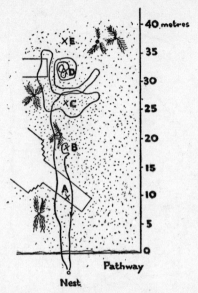

Fig. 15.—Tracks of wasps returning from various distances to their nest. They were successful in returning from points A–D (return tracks from A and C not shown to avoid confusion), none returned from E. (After Baerends.)

taken, the longer it takes to get back, largely because of the time spent on searching about before finding the way (fig. 15). There finally comes a point when it cannot find the way and unless it is

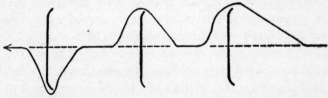

Fig. 16.—The track of a sand wasp when a screen was placed across its path in three successive positions. The wasp was running on the ground taking prey back to its nest. (After Thorpe.)

39

carried back on to familiar territory it is lost. By releasing a wasp
at different places and seeing whether it can home, a map can be
made of the area with which it is familiar.

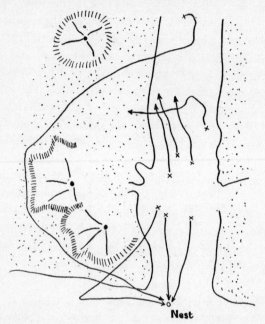

Nest

FIG. 17.—The return tracks of a wasp after being released at different places.
It returned directly from some points along the path but when released
farther away from its nest it made wide detours, one of which is shown
complete, going round the large trees. (After Baerends.)

It is comparatively easy for an animal to head straight towards
a desirable goal which remains in sight. Very different is the case
where an animal is able to make a detour around some obstacle,
leaving the direct path and even losing sight of its goal for a time,
yet finally returning. Another sand-wasp (*Ammophila pubescens*), a
close relative of the wasp we have just considered, can do this.
Dr. Thorpe put a screen in front of a female running back to her
nest with her prey and she ran round the obstacle and then
regained her original direction (fig. 16). He was able to do this
repeatedly, and each time the wasp avoided the screen. Most

remarkable, too, it did not simply run up to the screen and then follow round its edge, but started turning when it was still some distance away. It must have known the arrangement of the various landmarks very well to risk getting lost in this way.

Ammophila campestris, as we have seen, can recognize the landmarks again only after it has made an orientation flight. But men who learn their way about one district and then a neighbouring one can put their knowledge of the two together in their mind's eye and weld them into a map of the whole area. The wasp cannot do this. When taken away up one of the paths through the heathland, it would return along the path to its nest. But taken a little farther, it flew in a wide detour around some large trees even though it would have been much quicker and taken less effort to fly down the path (fig. 17). It seems as if the area in between was unknown, though the return route round the big trees from more distant places and the direct route back along the path from the nearer places were both well known. Able navigator though it is the wasp cannot piece together its fragments of knowledge and make a map!

CHAPTER IV

The Nectar Seekers

W E have seen how vital it is for social insects to return to their colonies, for without the food brought by the foragers the young die. We have also seen how ants travelling over the ground find their way, and how wasps learn to recognize their surroundings. But for thousands of years man has been concerned with another social insect, the honey-bee. Ever since primitive man first discovered the combs of wild bees laden with sweet honey (and there are cave paintings showing him taking them from trees), he has observed and remembered facts about the insects upon which his supplies of honey depend. As so frequently happens, his earliest observations were inaccurate, becoming further distorted into legends, now disproved, that were passed from one to another. Nowadays most countries have Government-supported research establishments whose work is entirely concerned with the study of hive bees, either *Apis indica* of the East, or the true honey-bee, *Apis mellifera* of the rest of the world. There now is a very great deal of information about the way of life of the honey-bee, but there is still a vast amount to learn.

Honey-bees are important pollinators. It is therefore useful to know what attracts them to particular flowers and what guides them in flight. It is also useful to know from what sort of flower they are likely to gather nectar, for all honey is not alike and many flowers give a distinctive flavour to the honey. Signs, such as colour, may be useful in guiding the bee to flowers and back to the hive and ensuring that as few foragers as possible are lost. Both bee-keeper and plant breeder want this information. With such an economic stimulus it is not surprising that so much information has been gained.

It was Sir John Lubbock, later Lord Avebury, who in the latter half of the nineteenth century investigated the colour sense of bees for the first time. He was a remarkable man, responsible for the reform of banking methods, the introduction of Bank Holidays and of laws to control the hours of shop assistants. But his interests also included entomology, archæology and literature. He showed that bees could learn to associate certain colours with food and to distinguish them from other colours. He laid out dishes of sugar syrup on squares of paper of one colour (say, blue) and placed squares of other colours on either side of them. After bees had visited the dishes he removed them and replaced them with clean empty ones; then he watched where the bees went and saw that they still returned to the blue papers, ignoring the other colours, thus demonstrating that the bees could not have been attracted by the scent of syrup, which was not there, but must have actually recognized the colour on which they had previously found food.

Unfortunately there was still one possibility which Lubbock had not considered. The bees might have been going to the papers which reflected a certain amount, not a certain kind, of light. In other words, they might have been attracted to darker or lighter papers, rather than to a colour. It remained for von Frisch, the justly celebrated German zoologist, to show for certain that bees really recognize colour. He arranged blue papers among papers of various shades of grey, some of them reflecting the same amount of light as the blue ones. He took every precaution to prevent the bees from using scent to guide them and still they visited the blue papers. By teaching the bees in this way to expect food on a patch of a particular colour he was able to show that they could distinguish between wavelengths of light which appear to us as yellow-orange, blue-green, blue-violet colours and ultra violet which, being invisible to us, has no name as a colour. Whereas we see the various wavelengths of visible light as a spectrum of seven colours blending into each other, the bee can discriminate only four colours in the light visible to it (fig. 18). It cannot see what we call red, which is interesting because the attractiveness of red flowers like harvest-poppies seems to argue against a blindness to red which seems general among other insects as well as bees. However, these particular flowers reflect a great deal of ultra violet light, which is the reason why bees are drawn to them. So it

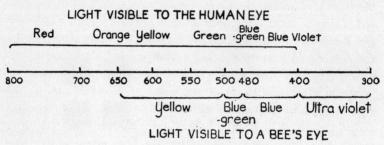

LIGHT VISIBLE TO THE HUMAN EYE

FIG. 18.—A comparison of the wavelengths of light visible to man and to honeybees.

is plain that once having found a source of abundant nectar or pollen a foraging bee can recognize it again later by its colour.

But we can also prove, as we could for the hunting wasp, that shapes with plenty of outline are more attractive to bees than ones which have less. It is difficult if not impossible for a bee to distinguish between a triangle and a circle if they are solid figures, but if they are simply outlines, they can be distinguished from each

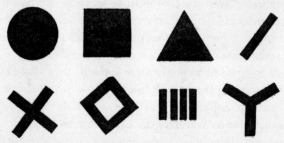

FIG. 19.—The figures in the top row could not be distinguished from each other by honey-bees but could be distinguished from any of those in the bottom row.

other. These contour figures have a longer outline than the solid ones; that is, there is a double boundary between black and white in these figures as opposed to the single one of the solid figures.

A bee will learn to come to a dish beside which is one of this second group, recognizing it among other shapes on subsequent visits (fig. 19). If we offer stars with different numbers of

FIG. 20.—When presented with these patterns without previous training, bees showed a preference for some of them. The percentage of choices made to each one in 226 tests are shown. (After Zerrahn.)

points, this time putting no food down at all, bees choose to visit those with the most points. They do this without training, so it seems that they have a natural preference for broken outlines and will choose the more indented shapes spontaneously. We can go on multiplying examples (fig. 20) and it becomes clear that the length or 'richness' of outline is the most important factor. A checkerboard pattern with many squares to a given area is preferred by bees to one with fewer squares, though they are larger. Bumble-bees have a very similar preference for long broken outlines (fig. 21).

FIG. 21.—Bumble-bees showed a natural preference for visiting the patterns in the bottom row when offered the choice between the pairs. Note that the total area of the small circles on the left is equal to the area of the circle above.

Checkerboard patterns are not natural, but star shapes are like the petal patterns of some flowers. Often these petals bear lines of colour which contrast with the rest; for instance, dark lines radiate outwards from the centre of a pansy. These are honey guides, in name as well as in fact. They usually point directly to the nectaries, which are often at the base of the petals. Contrasting patterns are more attractive to bees than those in which the colour of the background and the design are close, so that black shapes on a white ground are visited more frequently than the same shapes on a grey ground. The honey guides fulfil these conditions ideally, for the colours are often those which to the eye of a bee show a marked contrast and present an attractively long outline.

The stems of herbaceous plants are seldom rigid enough to hold the flowers motionless in the wind, and since moving patterns are more obvious than ones which are still, a pattern moving in the breeze has added attraction. It seems that a broken pattern attracts a bee because light from it flickers more rapidly on the individual parts of her eye, the changes in light stimulation of each segment being greater the more the pattern is broken up into light and dark parts (fig. 22). The faster the flicker, the more obvious it is. If the pattern itself moves, the speed of the flicker effect on the

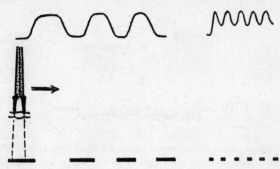

FIG. 22.—Diagram to show the flicker effect of two different patterns. The changes in stimulation of the ommatidium as it moves over the patterns from left to right are shown.

eye increases, particularly when the pattern is moving in the opposite direction to the bee. Thus the bee recognizes flowers by colour, shape, length of outline and flicker effect, as well as by their scent, so that she can return to them if they are giving a good nectar flow or contain much pollen.

Oddly enough, a bee does not learn the appearance of a food locality as she leaves, but as she approaches. This has been proved by experiment. A dish of sugar syrup is put out on top of a pile of differently coloured or differently patterned papers. Then we wait for a bee to visit it. As soon as she alights we can pull away the top paper to reveal the one below it, which has a different colour or a different shape painted on it. Then, when she is preparing to fly off, we pull away the second paper to show yet another (fig. 23). After she has gone back to the hive and returns to the dish we repeat the process, starting with the same colour or shape. But after a few times we confront her with the three different colours, or shapes, side by side, all without sugar syrup. We then see that the bee circles the paper similar to that which she saw when she first flew towards the dish, ignoring those seen while drinking or when flying away.

Nevertheless, when she flies away to return to the hive, the forager circles over the feeding place. The purpose of this flight is to learn how the feeding place fits in with the surroundings and to

FIG. 23.—Three papers are arranged under a dish of sugar-water so that they may be withdrawn one after the other to expose different patterns of colours at different times.

learn the look of the neighbouring objects which will serve as landmarks when she approaches once again.

But a bee makes a similar orientation flight on another occasion—when she leaves her hive. Then she flies out, turns towards the hive entrance and flies in vertical circles in front of it. She fixes the position of her home in her memory at that moment. And if while she is away foraging the hive is moved she comes back to the point in space where the hive entrance used to be, and searches for it there. Even if the hive is only turned round she does not find the entrance immediately but alights where the entrance used to be and wanders about on the hive wall until she crawls round the corner and happens to find the entrance in its new position. For several subsequent returns she will land on the wall and run round to the entrance, though later she begins to fly straight there.

Now we can get some idea of how a bee learns the position of her hive and the position of the flowers from which she collects food. Indeed, the characteristics by which she recognizes the flowers are also those by which she recognizes the landmarks. The hive itself is a landmark and if hives are painted with different colours, fewer bees 'drift' into the wrong hives when they are set close together, provided that the colours are chosen to correspond with those which a bee sees. The hive is the beginning of a bee's journey and the flowers the end of it. The insect cannot often see the one when she leaves the other, only rarely can she fly towards either with her goal in sight. She has therefore to navigate by means of intermediate landmarks and beacons which have no direct connection with either end of her journey. Thus the trees or houses that she may recognize are not necessarily those next to the hive or around her feeding place, but merely line the route.

These landmarks are very influential. On one occasion hives were put out on a disused aerodrome, a large expanse of ground uninterrupted by any obvious features. Various objects were placed on the ground along the line of flight of bees as they flew from the hive to a feeding dish. After a time these objects were moved sideways and the bees followed, flying along the new line though it led them astray.

Yet sometimes in the same experiments the bees would fly in the same compass direction wherever they were. Some of the workers had been foraging at a dish some distance from the hive and had been flying directly back again. While some were feeding, the dish was moved a distance sideways. When the bees flew off they did not turn towards the hive but flew on a course parallel to the first (fig. 24). This happened even if the dish was placed on the opposite side of the hive, so that by flying in the old direction they actually flew away from their hive. We shall see later that young migrating birds will also maintain their course after they have been moved away from their route (p. 106); the result is the same though the reasons are no doubt different.

After the bees had flown a distance which was approximately equivalent to the original distance from dish to hive they started circling, searching apparently for the non-existent alighting board. This result was baffling, for despite the lack of landmarks the bees could navigate and maintain an absolute compass direction. That they could see distant features on the horizon seemed unlikely, though at the time there seemed to be no other explanation. However, in 1949 Professor von Frisch clearly showed that bees can and do use the pattern of light from the sky to guide themselves.

Provided that at least some part of the sky is free from cloud, and even on occasions when the sky is quite overcast, bees can find their way without reference to landmarks on the ground. Here

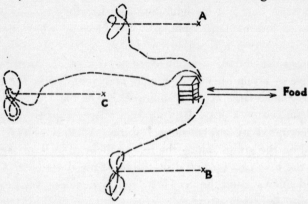

FIG. 24.—Bees which had been collecting food as shown on the right were moved while feeding to A, B or C. Typical tracks from these points are shown. They all flew in the correct direction and for approximately the right distance before searching for their hive. (After Wolf.)

was the explanation of how the bees on the aerodrome could navigate without visible landmarks.

Light consists of waves which we can imagine like those which travel along a rope when one end is quickly moved up and down, the waves being vertical in direction. But the waves comprising ordinary light are not all vertical; some are horizontal and the remainder inclined at all angles across the direction of the ray, so that seen end on the vibrations crossing the x axis at all angles would look like this:

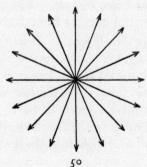

When light is reflected from, say the surface of the sea or the thin film of water on a wet road, a large proportion of it is *polarized*. This means that only those waves in which the vibrations

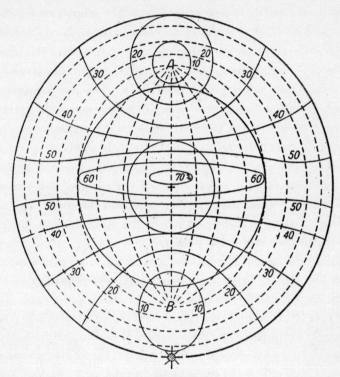

SUN ON HORIZON

FIG. 25.—Distribution of polarized light over the sky, when the sun is on the horizon. The solid lines indicate the points of equal percentage of polarization and the broken lines point where the angle of polarization is the same. A and B are the two points where the light is unpolarized. The diagram represents the hemisphere of the sky, + being the highest point and the two rings concentric with + being the lines subtending angles of 30 deg. and 60 deg. with the horizontal. (After Müller-Pouillet.)

are in one direction—for example, vertically across the beam—are reflected. This is known as *plane-polarized light*. Actually, not all the light which is reflected from water or a mirror is polarized, for the proportion varies according to the angle of the ray with the surface of the reflector. The light which leaves the sun is not polarized at first but when the rays strike particles in the outer atmosphere (those which give the sky its blue colour) part of the light is scattered as plane-polarized light. The proportion which is polarized in this way varies in different parts of the sky and the angle of the plane of polarization is not the same over the whole of the sky's hemisphere. There is a regular pattern of percentage of polarization and angle of polarization over the hemisphere which is related to the sun. Thus, as the sun moves the pattern moves with it, and any point where there is a particular percentage of the light polarized at a particular angle will bear a constant relationship to the sun (fig. 25). To use this pattern as a guide all that is required is a device for measuring these two factors. Unfortunately some kinds of cloud upset this pattern because the light is scattered in a different way by the water droplets, though other types of cloud act as polarizers.

Most of us cannot discern this pattern unless we have a special filter to help us. There are a number of ways of making such a filter but the plastic Polaroid is one of the easiest to use. The action of all these filters is to allow only the light waves which are vibrating in one particular plane to pass. If we imagine the filter as being like a very narrow slit which permits the vibrating wave to pass through only if the slit is parallel to the wave, we shall have some idea of how it functions. For if we look at plane-polarized light through one of these filters we see the light at its brightest with the filter held in a given position, but as we turn it the light diminishes until, when we have turned it through a right-angle, it seems to be extinguished, increasing in intensity again as the filter continues to be turned. We can produce polarized light by shining ordinary light through one of these filters, for all the waves are excluded except those vibrating in the plane of the filter, all those, that is, that are not vibrating in the plane of the slit.

When a worker bee, having found an abundant supply of food, returns to the hive she performs a dance which communicates the whereabouts of the food to other foragers waiting in the hive. If

 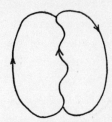

FIG. 26.—The dances of successful foragers which have returned to the hive. Left, the round dance performed when the food source is less than 100 metres from the hive. Right, the waggle-tail figure-of-eight dance performed when the food lies farther from the hive. (After von Frisch.)

the food is less than 100 metres away, the bee performs a round dance (fig. 26), but if it is further away the dancer performs a figure-of-eight, tail wagging movement (fig. 26). There are transitional dances between these two, in which the two overlapping circles of the round dance are gradually moved away from each other until they lie side by side to form the figure-of-eight. Very little information is given to the foragers by the round dance, simply that the food is within 100 metres from the hive, though combined with all these dances is information about the kind of flowers that has been found; their scent will be on the bee's body and in the nectar or pollen some of which the interested would-be recruits receive from her, while the scent with which the finder may have marked her treasure will also be detected by them. But the figure-of-eight dance gives more information, showing the direction as well as the distance of the food.

The dances are usually performed on the vertical face of the comb in the complete darkness within the hive, though we can observe them through the glass wall of an observation hive. They continue to be performed even when we watch them in red light, to which bees are not sensitive, which is very convenient for the observer. As the dancing bee moves along the middle of the figure-of-eight she waggles her abdomen from side to side, the number of wags being proportionate to the distance which she flew (fig. 27). This distance is measured apparently by the

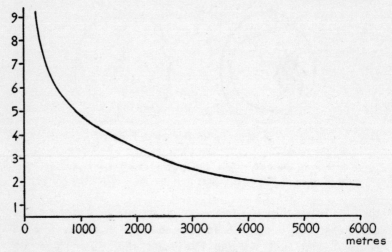

FIG. 27.—The relationship between the distance from hive to food and the number of abdomen waggles in a quarter of a second when the bee dances. Distance along the horizontal, and number of waggles along the vertical axis. (After von Frisch.)

exertion of the bee in flying to the food, for if she has to battle against a headwind the distance she indicates on her return is greater than the real distance, and if she is speeded along by a following wind the distance is shorter than the real one. The direction of this waggle dance indicates the direction in which the food lies. For this the force of gravity is substituted for the direction of the sun, so that a dance which goes straight up the comb indicates that the food is in the direction of the sun and a dance straight down shows that the foraging bee must head away from the sun to reach it. A dance at an angle to the vertical means that the bee must fly in a direction at that angle to the left or right of the sun (fig. 28). When the bee dances on the alighting board, which it sometimes does, in this horizontal position it heads along the middle part of the figure in the direction of the food. On one occasion bees had to make a detour around the shoulder of a mountain, so that their flight to the food was not direct (fig. 29); yet their dances indicated the true direction, the way in which a

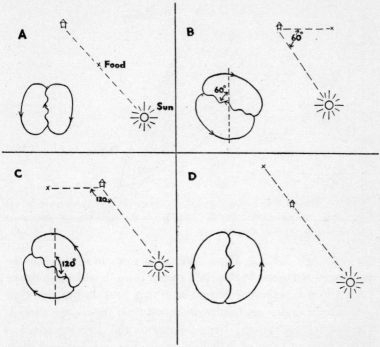

FIG. 28.—Diagram to show how the direction of the dance on the vertical face of the comb is related to the direction of food source and sun. In A, the food lies in the direction of the sun, in B, at 60 deg. to it, in C, at 120 deg. to it and in D, in the opposite direction. (After von Frisch.)

crow would fly but not a bee. There seems to be no explanation for this and it is not clear how the foragers who followed the dancer interpreted it. Height cannot be indicated in the dance. This was proved when a hive was put at the bottom of a radio mast and the food was hauled to the top of it directly above the hive. Though the foragers found the food their dance language was unable to signify the position; the dancers were 'speechless' and danced chaotically.

Thus the bee must know the position of the sun, though it will forage and dance on days when the sky is almost covered by cloud. When the sky is completely overcast few bees leave the hive and

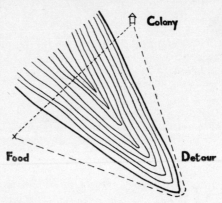

FIG. 29.—Though the bees flew round the mountain spur (a distance of 149 metres) they indicated the direction across the spur (shorter dashes) in their dance. (After von Frisch.)

there are few dancers. But as long as part of the sky is clear the pattern of polarized light which comes from it will indicate the sun's position. It seems certain now that bees do use this light pattern, for if it is artificially disturbed their dances are altered. For example, some bees were dancing on the alighting board in front of the entrance of their hive, which was in a darkened shed. As they danced their figures-of-eight they headed in the direction in which lay the food they had found. They only danced, however, when a wide tube open at both ends was put through the roof of the shed, its lower end over the bees so that through it the dancers could see blue sky, though not the sun itself. A polarized light filter was placed over the upper end and when it was turned the dancers turned too, shifting the direction of their figures through the same angle. This showed that the direction of their dance was influenced by the pattern of polarized light which they could see through the tube.

Von Frisch now went further. He wanted to discover how the bee was able to determine the sky light pattern, so he made a device of eight triangular pieces of Polaroid forming an octagon. When he looked through it at the sky in various directions he found that he could see different patterns of light and dark in the

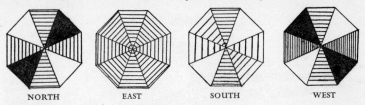

NORTH   EAST   SOUTH   WEST

FIG. 30.—Four different patterns observed at the same time of day when the sky was viewed in various directions through an artificial eye constructed of Polaroid, depth of shading represents amount of light. (After von Frisch.)

octagon at different parts of the sky or in the same part of the sky at different times of day (fig. 30). He used this device to look at what the dancing bees in the shed were seeing when the polaroid at the end of the tube was turned. As the filter turned, the pattern on his octagon changed; sometimes the new pattern was the same as the one from another part of the sky and indeed the bees took up a new direction which would have been correct if that other part had been overhead. But if the pattern he saw when the polaroid was turned was not one he could identify anywhere in the sky, then the bees danced in a chaotic way with no particular direction. Apparently because what they saw was confusing, their dance was also confused and erratic.

A bee's eye is composed of units, the ommatidia, in each of which is a set of eight sensitive cells packed round a central rod which bends the light passing into it so that the rays enter the sensitive cells (fig. 31). The octagon of polaroid pieces seems to echo this arrangement. There are also some physiological experiments which make it fairly clear that it is in the sensitive cells, not in any other part of the ommatidium, that the analysis of the polarized light pattern is carried out. Probably the segments of the central rod, the rhabdome, which has eight parts, one corresponding to and perhaps produced by each sensitive cell, are the real analysers, functioning like the polaroid filters which have already been mentioned.

When we come to consider how the information is derived, encoded as it were, picked up by another bee and used for navigation, we see how complex the process is. Suppose it is a

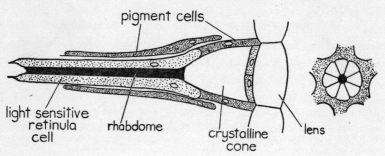

pigment cells

light sensitive
retinula
cell

rhabdome

crystalline
cone

lens

FIG. 31.—A diagrammatic longitudinal section of an ommatidium of an insect's eye. On the right, a cross section of the sensitive retinulae cells and the rhabdome.

cloudy day, and the sun is hidden; the returning bee sees a certain pattern of light in the segments of her left eye. From this she can apparently tell the position of the sun she cannot see. This position is represented in her brain, and the angle her line of flight makes with it is connected in some way with her sensitivity to gravity, so that when she dances she performs at an equal angle to the vertical. A bee trails across the comb after her and in the follower's brain the angle made by her own track with the direction of gravity is perceived and turned into some kind of memory trace, so that when she leaves the hive, she can navigate on the correct bearing to the sun. But the sun may still be hidden, in which case the bee must turn herself until the correct pattern of light falls on the correct segments of her eye. It does seem possible that much of this could be explained by invoking a fairly simple nervous mechanism for the translation of the various pieces of information into terms of other senses, but learning certainly adds greatly to these automatic mechanisms. Obviously the light pattern which guides the bee back to the hive and will also guide a forager out from the hive to the food has to be learned. Also we have only dealt with the information concerning direction, we have ignored distance and scent identification of the food which increase still further the amount of information which is passed by the dancer to the forager which runs behind. And we now know that bees, using their sense of time, compensate for the movement of the sky pattern during the day. The complexity of the interconnections between the parts of the bee's brain responsible for vision, scent and gravity sense must be very great.

We know that ants too can perceive polarized light and make use of the sky pattern to guide themselves. We know that ants can alter their orientation from one at an angle to a light beam into one at the same angle to gravity. But ant workers do not perform a dance as do bees; they do not communicate information in the detailed way that a bee does. It seems that the most they can do is to indicate to other workers by their quick movements and by regurgitation of the contents of their crop that they have found food.

The ability to recognize polarized light is being established in more and more animals, though so far none of them are outside the group of the hard-bodied animals, the arthropods, which includes insects, spiders, crabs and their allies. Some insects, like the caterpillars of a pine sawfly, use the sky light pattern to keep their tracks straight by moving almost literally with one eye on the sky. They do not head towards any particular place but merely use this beacon as a means of wandering in a straight line. We have already noted that it is probably better for an animal to go straight ahead rather than to circle or to zig-zag for it is more likely to encounter new sources of food and so forth.

There is a sand hopper on the seashore which stays on the belt of wet sand above the wash of the sea. When the hoppers are put on the dry sand higher up the shore, they make their way straight back to the wet area which they prefer. Apparently they guide themselves by the light from the sky. Hoppers from the west coast of Italy transported and set free on the eastern shores still hopped westward in their endeavour to reach the sea though in their new locality this was quite the wrong way to go. Hoppers in a bowl will jump in the direction of the sea, but they alter their direction when a polarized light filter held over the bowl changes the pattern presented to their eyes.

Probably this ability to perceive polarized light, and more particularly to analyse it, is bound up with the structure of the arthropod compound eye, though this cannot be the whole story, as the caterpillars of the pine sawflies have simple eyes constructed on a plan different from that of the compound eyes of adult insects. Nevertheless these eyes still have refractive bodies in them which may function in the same way as the central rod of an ommatidium of a compound eye. Perhaps we shall never discover an animal without a hard body and jointed limbs possessing this remarkable and, to us, novel ability.

CHAPTER V

At the Mercy of the Elements

INSECTS, in making their journeys, may range far from the places where they emerged from their eggs, and often they never return to their birthplaces, but, unlike birds, fly on until they die. In 1924 literally millions of painted-lady butterflies were seen flying roughly northwards in California; one estimate put the number of travellers as 3,000,000,000 spread out in a band forty miles wide. And in Africa and the Middle East every year somewhere the sky is blackened by vast swarms of locusts which descend on crops and devour them. Sometimes all kinds of insects make up these moving bands. Dr. William Beebe, the well-known American naturalist of the tropics, stood on a mound in Portachuelo Pass in Venezuela and watched a great mass of insects moving southward through the pass. He and his companions counted, for example, an average of 1,300 ten-spot butterflies passing every four minutes. 'In the narrow trail above the gorge it was necessary to put on glasses, so dense were the crowds impinging on our faces.' No less than fifteen orders of insects were represented in these flying columns, with butterflies and moths, beetles, true flies, wasps and bees the most abundant (plate 6).

We do not know what causes all these mass movements, but we do know sufficient of the biology of a few insects which move about, sometimes in great numbers, to attempt an explanation in their cases. It seems that some of these movements are the result of such an increase in numbers that over-population of their habitat threatens exhaustion of food supplies. Some leave the area, often in large numbers, to spill out into the surrounding countryside. The same reason probably lies behind the movements of lemmings.

Thus the animals do not alternate regularly between two areas, nor does the whole population necessarily move at the same time. Both of these characteristics are diametrically opposite to two of the essentials of what has been described as 'true migration,' best typified by bird migration. Our insects escaping the threat of food shortage have therefore been described to be 'emigrating' and not migrating. But we shall see that locusts, to give one example only, do move back and forth between two general areas on some occasions, while the migrations of the bogong moth are very like those of birds in that the moths breed in only one of the two places they visit. With our increasing knowledge of the reasons and the ways of insect migration it becomes less and less easy to describe insect movements definitely as migration or emigration. So we shall not concern ourselves further with this distinction; what matters is how far some form of navigation is involved.

On most occasions the whole of one of these great bands is moving in the same direction, for either individual differences in heading are ironed out because of the controlling effect of the close proximity of large numbers of their fellows, or the members of the band may be healthy individualists, as it were, orientating separately but in the same direction, uninfluenced by their companions. The behaviour of the flock may not necessarily be the same as the behaviour of any one of the individuals isolated from the rest. The ants, the hunting wasps and bees just mentioned could each navigate for themselves, and individual butterflies and locusts can also do so, but when they fly in a flock new factors may prevent them straying from the swarm. It may appear that they are being led by individuals of higher intelligence and navigational abilities; in fact they almost certainly are not. Relatively few migratory animals do follow leaders, rather each navigates for itself, the direction they take up being modified by a strong tendency to keep together. If they tend to fly out of the swarm, their desire to keep with their companions draws them back again, just as wanderers were brought back into the columns of the army ants by their desire to touch and smell their companions—but for different reasons, of course. Swarms of locusts and flocks of butterflies are probably governed by these principles. Of other insects that are seen in plague bands and fly long distances—aphids, beetles, etc.—very little, or nothing at all is known of the causes of their migration and their means of navigation.

From the times when large-scale cultivation was first undertaken by primitive man in Africa, the Middle East and India, plagues of locusts have been feared, for in their wake came famine. Primitive agriculture does not include allowance for bad times and when a crop fails there are rarely any reserves to fall back on. There are many ancient references to these plagues. Locusts figure in the Old Testament both as a food and as a scourge. They appear on the walls of Egyptian tombs. An Assyrian bas-relief pays tribute to their value for the table for they are being brought to King Asurbinipal as part of his supper. The succulent females, full of eggs, remain a delicacy to this day. But the ancients also recognized the importance of control measures. In Roman North Africa there were stringent regulations, the purpose of which was to reduce the damage done by them.

More recently locust damage throughout the world has been estimated at £30,000,000 each year. Spurred on by the economic consequences of locust invasions the nations concerned have banded together to form an international locust control office. As a result of this a great deal is known about the different kinds of locust and their behaviour, though this has perhaps served to turn what appeared to be a simple picture into one of bewildering complexity, and there are many gaps in our knowledge.

Locusts lay their eggs in the soil, and they hatch as nymphs, small editions of the adults, though their wings are not fully developed. Through the subsequent months the earth-bound hoppers, as the nymphs are called, grow larger until finally they are transformed into fully-winged adults. The hoppers march and jump across the countryside in huge bands while the adults fill the sky with their swarms. Both adults and young cause damage. A recent plague of the migratory locust will serve as an example of how the swarms develop and move. Small swarms were first noticed in the area of the River Niger in 1926 and 1927. By 1928 the swarms had grown, aided no doubt by particularly suitable

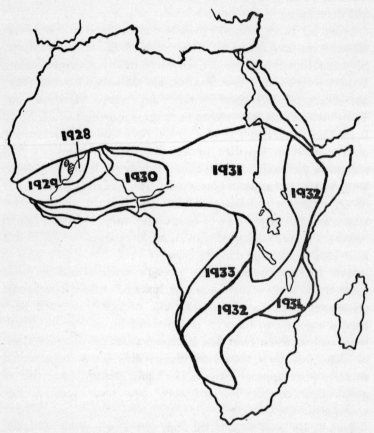

Fig. 32.—The spread of the migratory locust from the Niger flood plains where it was first observed in 1927–28 (cross-hatched areas) to other parts of Africa in the succeeding years. (After Uvarov.)

conditions. As this locust usually produces two broods a year the growth of a large population can be reasonably quick. Indeed by 1930 swarms covered West Africa south of the Sahara and spread across the continent as far as Lake Chad (fig. 32). Vast numbers were produced in the same year and began to migrate eastwards, penetrating into the Anglo-Egyptian Sudan. During the next few years the locusts travelled south-westwards to invade South West Africa, having covered a good part of Kenya and Tanganyika. Unfortunately for the locusts their entry into southern Africa coincided with the dry season. They also flew out to sea in large numbers. By the end of 1935 the plagues had died down in East and Central Africa though the West African plague centre continued to produce recruits which in 1940 spread to the east, once again entering Kenya and Tanganyika. But for some reason, after this flash in the pan the numbers of the locust were drastically reduced to below plague proportions throughout the area.

This outbreak was fairly typical in that the swarms moved across country without any apparent goal, taking advantage of any local conditions of the right humidity and so forth to land and lay eggs. There were a series of generations, twenty-five in all, which covered the ground like the successive runners in a relay team handing the baton on to the next. They did not make their way to any particular place, for many parts of the country can become suitable for egg-laying if the local climatic conditions, particularly humidity, are favourable. The plague which we have described stemmed from the River Niger flood plains, which is an area where the conditions frequently encourage the growth of a population and the formation of swarms. But although the swarms did not apparently head for particular places, some of them in later generations were swept back towards the areas from which their grandparents came.

Does this mean that they can navigate? It might be that they are carried by the prevailing winds of the particular season and that they return along an earlier route only because the wind happens to be in the right direction. But this does not always hold true. The overall trend of locust swarms is with the prevailing wind but their path on occasions may be into or across this wind. In fact since breeding takes place at different seasons the winds which could influence the swarms are likely to be different. It is not at all clear at first how wind does influence the direction the fliers take.

The desert locust, for example, occurs over northern India, the whole of the Middle East and throughout Africa north of the Equator, spreading southward to Tanganyika on the eastern seaboard. A generation is produced during the monsoon rains in the southern part of this vast area. The insects hatch and, when adult, fly northwards, laying eggs in winter and spring in the north which hatch in their turn. The adults of this second generation then move southwards, breeding in the monsoon rains of the south, so that a population is in the southern area once again, though it is now composed of individuals different from those of the previous year. A large percentage of swarms drift south or south-west under the influence of the north-east monsoon in December to February. Their northward movement is carried out against the prevailing wind though they return on the prevailing wind. Occasionally an unusually strong wind may carry locusts beyond their normal range. Large swarms of desert locusts were seen in Portugal in October 1945, having apparently been swept out to sea off southern Morocco and carried northwards, since swarms had not been seen to pass overland by French observers in Morocco. The distance covered was about 800 miles, compared with the normal average daily migration of 20 to 30 miles. Their speedy transit seems to have been made at about 2,000 feet, where a fast moving wind carried them at an average speed of 22 to 26 m.p.h. Normally they would settle at night, but ascending air currents and the fact that they were over the sea prevented them from doing so. Individual locusts have been blown out to the Azores and northwards to the British Isles.

These are doubtless extreme cases but they do show the power of the wind as a factor in controlling locust movement. Nevertheless, they can navigate, and they control the direction in which they fly at a given moment, though this does not affect the overall drift of the swarms.

In the morning the swarms which have been resting on the ground and on trees and bushes begin to become active. Before the locusts can fly they need to be warmed up, and each locust aligns itself across the sun's rays, presenting its body broadside to the warming rays. As the sun rises so the locusts tip over so that their bodies continue to present the greatest possible area to the sun. When the body temperature has risen sufficiently, the insects turn away, often standing with their heads towards the sun so that as little as possible is now warmed. A few glide down from the trees to the ground, making little or no headway. More scatter to the ground. Then a few start to flutter, and others being now sufficiently warmed, join in. A thin cloud of insects begins to circle and weave above the rest of the swarm still basking in the sun. Those which are flying land and take off again at short intervals. But gradually they fly more and more strongly, drawing in more and more of their fellows, until large flocks fly short distances, only to wheel down to the ground again. They fly in various directions, but by now the main trend is becoming accentuated until finally the flocks aggregate and stream away in one direction, the thin rattle of their wings filling the watcher's ears as the multitude darkens the sky. The swarm is thick, some insects flying just above the ground while others are at a hundred feet or more. This is the general distribution but up-currents may carry locusts higher, some having been seen at 7,000 feet.

Dr. J. S. Kennedy has suggested that vision must have much to do with the individual's navigation. A locust sees the countryside reeling past beneath it and so long as it is making headway the images pass from in front of its eye backwards, just as when we look out of a train window. But if images start going the other way, the locust probably turns downwind so that it is swept along; then the images will once again pass in the direction which the locust seems to prefer. But images passing from behind forwards must be an anathema. This at any rate is one possible explanation, and observation seems to support it. Locusts fly at an average of about 4 metres per second and if close to the ground manage to maintain their direction in headwinds of lower speeds. When the windspeed rises and equals their flying speed they apparently become confused, if they are near the ground, and as it rises further tend to turn downwind, until at windspeeds of about

8 metres per second and above they settle. Presumably at such higher speeds images move faster than they like.

Those which travel in the upper layers of the swarm are less efficient at keeping direction than those lower down. An explanation for this is that the higher the insect flies the less quickly the images move across its eyes and indeed the less distinct are small objects on the ground. When the windspeed increases locusts tend to fly lower, thus actually emphasizing the movement of the images. At lower levels, also, the windspeed is reduced by the friction with the ground.

One might well ask why a flying insect should not be able to take its direction from that of the wind; but to do this it would have to sense the direction of the wind while flying, a problem which affects all flying animals and to which we shall return when we consider bird navigation. It is quite plain that any flying animal becomes part of the moving air, for it is supported by it. The only pressure it feels on its body is caused by its own forward movement. If it is travelling downwind as fast as or faster than the wind that is carrying it there will be no pressure upon its head and it will certainly not be able to sense the direction of the wind. But this argument only applies if the speed of the wind is absolutely uniform—a steady stream of air—which is unusual, for most winds blow in gusts. These gusts are stretched out along the direction of the wind, so that if the orientation of the gusts could be sensed, a flying animal could get some idea of the direction of the supporting wind. It happens that there are hairs on the locust's forehead which are sensitive to air flow, so that if air strikes a stationary insect's head from the side instead of from ahead, it turns into the airstream. Perhaps by using these receptors a locust could sense the direction of the gusts while in free flight, but there is no evidence that they do so.

Other observations show what a relatively minor direct role wind plays in orientating a swarm. This is very well demonstrated when locusts fly over water. On one occasion a swarm took off from a lake shore when the wind dropped and flew over the lake into what little wind there was, but when they had gone a mile or so out over the water the wind rose and blew them back. They were tumbled back in disorder, keeping their height; this is quite unlike the behaviour of a swarm advancing over land, which turns in an orderly manner downwind when the wind rises. They did not seem to perceive that they were being swept backwards. Unlike the countryside on its perimeter the lake surface would be an expanse without landmarks so the swarm was being effectively deprived of the very means by which it could navigate visually. The locusts were apparently unable to compensate for the wind under those conditions, for their perception of wind normally comes indirectly, through the drift which the wind imposes on them.

One other factor should not be overlooked: the ever-present landmark of the sun itself. It is difficult to get reliable evidence that a great band of flying insects is maintaining a constant angle to the direction of the sun's rays as ants do. But Kennedy did manage to make some flying locusts turn completely round when he shaded them from the direct sun and simultaneously reflected it upon them from the opposite direction. He was able to direct bands of marching hoppers in this way as they moved across country. So the possibility of sun navigation playing its part, as might well be expected, should not be excluded, though it clearly acts in concert with, but subordinate to response to moving images.

The picture which emerges from all this is of individual locusts being able to navigate and thus maintain a definite direction for short distances at least, provided they are close to the ground and the windspeed is not so great that they turn down wind or settle. But they do not always keep close to the ground, and the final general displacement of a swarm over a period of weeks coincides fairly well with the prevailing winds. When there is disagreement it is because the winds have not been mainly in that direction during that period. The problem arises, however, as to how the locusts choose the direction which they first take up and maintain for a short time. This direction does not necessarily bear any relationship to the eventual goal, as the members of the swarm may at any one moment be heading in a very different direction from that of the whole swarm (plate 7). It is thus unnecessary and foolish to postulate any innate sense of direction for locusts. At first, no doubt, the individuals turn into the wind when they take off in the morning. Aerodynamically this is the most favourable way to become airborne. This direction is maintained as far as possible, the insect being held to its way by navigation by landmarks, the sun and so forth, but alterations in windspeed or some other factor may cause it to alter its heading.

It may help us to look at the migrations of other insects, and in particular butterflies, to see whether these give us any explanation. These migrations are not isolated phenomena, some fifty out of the 200 to 300 species of butterflies throughout the world are migratory. The migrations are regular and annual, though they may not always be as obvious, for the number of butterflies taking part varies widely. Many other butterflies are known to make directional flights each season, though whether these species make return flights at some other season is not known. Otherwise the pattern in the northern hemisphere is like that of birds, a northward trek at the beginning of the summer and a southward one in the autumn. Though the spring journey is undertaken by large numbers concentrated into a huge flock, the southward migration is often more diffuse, the fliers being spread over a larger area. Consequently the spring flight is more obvious than the autumn. Indeed, the southward journey has still to be observed in a number of butterflies which are known to make the earlier journey and very probably return in the autumn.

Unlike migratory birds, butterflies breed at both ends of their annual journeys. Painted ladies, for example, breed in Africa, north of the Sahara, during the winter and move northwards crossing the Mediterranean into Europe to lay eggs occasionally as far north as the north of Scotland. It is the insects which come from these eggs that make the return journey southwards; their parents do not see Africa again. The existence of a southward migration of painted ladies is still not certain, though a few have been seen heading south across the Mediterranean. In all probability the numbers flying south are much smaller than those flying north which again does not help observers searching for evidence of migration. However, a most striking autumnal migration of insects is to be seen in some of the passes of the Pyrenees. Here the insects group together to fly up the passes and become more conspicuous than when spread out over the country-side.

Even the numbers of painted ladies in the spring stream are not constant. In the spring, following the phenomenal Californian migration already mentioned, one observer saw only two butterflies, but there were conspicuous migrations again in 1926, 1941 and 1945, which lasted for about two months, often covering a front of 200 miles or more. All the butterflies of this kind, wherever they are found in the United States, apparently stem from Western Mexico, for there are no reports of major breeding areas elsewhere. But painted ladies found in Newfoundland do not themselves make the journey of 3,000 miles. Those that start the journey lay eggs *en route* which give rise to butterflies that cover the next lap of the journey. No one in America has seen an autumnal southward movement but probably, as in Europe, no one has looked in the right places.

But another common American butterfly has been seen to make autumn and spring flights in opposite directions. The North American race of the milkweed butterfly is found all over the States and southern Canada, spreading southwards into Central America and the northern parts of the Gulf of Mexico. These butterflies make massed flights in the autumn, small groups forming at first and joining together into conspicuous swarms later, all heading south. They seem to avoid the highlands of the Rockies but spread out over the West Coast, and continental America on the eastern side of the mountain backbone. Their flights end in Florida and California, where they hang in festoons on trees which may be the roosting posts of butterflies year after year. With the warmth of spring, they begin to fly and mate, heading northwards and laying eggs as they go. Finally, after two or three months and as many generations, the butterflies appear in the northernmost parts of their range. Here the last generation of the year develops, producing the adults which will fly south in the great bands of autumn. So at least some of the adults which begin the spring journey have already experienced the southward one, unlike the locusts and perhaps the painted ladies, in which a new generation makes each of the journeys.

These are just two examples from the huge amount of material on the migration of butterflies which has been collected and sifted by Dr. C. B. Williams. Thanks to him we now know that butterflies and many other insects do in fact migrate and in many cases make a double journey like birds.

But one of the many problems that remain is: how do they find their way? How can they be so accurate in their flight that the same trees may be roosts for milkweed butterflies winter after winter? The straight flight of these insects is most striking. Dr. Williams has himself described white butterflies which in East Africa flew up to the wall of his house, up to the roof, along it and down the other side in the persistence of their south-easterly direction. Painted ladies have been seen to cross a ravine by flying down one side and up the other rather than make a direct crossing from lip to lip—not unlike those birds which have been seen to descend when they reach a cliff edge, so that they flew on at the same height above the ensuing country-side as above the cliff top. Their navigation has a bewildering certainty about it. Milkweed butterflies were once seen flying south over part of Lake Ontario, when at a certain point the stream turned east for a hundred yards and then turned southwards once again. Even though the stream was not continuous and there were times when no butterflies were passing overhead, the next batch to arrive manœuvred in the same way, turning at the same points (fig. 33). Nothing in the weather conditions or the configuration of the lake shore could give a clue to the way in which these points were marked or why the insects turned at all.

Indeed one cannot help speculating on the reason for butterfly migration in general. Probably by avoiding the high summer temperatures which they would encounter in their winter quarters they are able to reproduce more efficiently. The availability of food is certainly of great importance. The bogong moths of south-eastern Australia leave the pastures in the southern

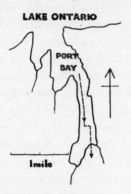

Fig. 33.—The track of butterflies migrating over Port Bay, Lake Ontario. (After Williams.)

spring to make their way to the mountains, where they pass the summer in a state of æstivation, waking in the autumn to fly down the mountains back to the pasture. In spring grasses begin to dominate the pasture land to the detriment of the herbs which are the moth's food, but they give place to herbs once again in the autumn. So the migration seems to be connected with the disappearance and reappearance of food.

Compared with locusts, butterflies and moths are relatively unimportant from an economic point of view, which accounts in a large measure for the relative lack of knowledge about the behaviour of the butterflies in the migratory swarms. It is certain wind does not control a butterfly's flight in the way that it affects the general displacement of a locust swarm. They are not carried passively by the wind and indeed it is questionable whether any migratory insects are. For they do not always fly with the wind and on many occasions butterflies have been seen flying across the wind at various angles, and even flying against it. Like locusts, in some cases at least, they appear to adjust their height according to the wind, flying low in a headwind and higher in a following wind. This makes one suspect that perhaps the same sort of mechanism is at work as in the locusts, that is, the influence of moving images enabling the fliers to judge whether they are making headway or being swept back. We know nothing of the abilities of butterflies to judge wind direction. They will continue to maintain a straight course even when the tropical sun is directly overhead, so that the use of the sun itself as a guiding beacon at that time seems unlikely. No experiments with mirrors have been done on these insects. Nevertheless the sun may have some function still to be discovered, for an inference that sun navigation plays no part at one time of the day does not imply that it is not used at other times. We simply do not know. But it is very likely that a multiplicity of methods are in use, so that if the sun is obscured some other indications of position come into play.

In these examples of insects flying persistently in one direction for a long period, we seem to have further evidence of the use of various natural beacons to correct any deviation from a heading previously taken up. No sense of direction need be implied or invoked, the original heading may be dependent upon some natural factor operating at the moment of take-off, just as locusts first fly upwind. The insect does not need to head towards a goal, for the locusts and butterflies have generally never been to the places they ultimately reach, and locusts do not in fact head for any fixed place. They merely fly actively and are carried long distances only by particular winds. The relative inflexibility of the routes is a measure of the unchanging character of the meteorological and climatic conditions and not of some fixed inherited route which every locust or butterfly knows, or of some memories of a golden Utopia to which every migrating insect strives.

CHAPTER VI

The Migrations of Birds

༈

ONE of the signs of autumn is the lines of swallows
perched wing to wing along the telephone wires and roof
tops. Within a few days they are all gone, and are not seen
again until their return the following spring. Some of the
migratory birds do not stay with us long:

> The cuckoo comes in April,
> She sings a song in May,
> In June she beats upon the drum,
> And then she'll fly away.

All that most people observe is that birds are in one place at one
season but not there at any other time. Indeed the older naturalists
did not always connect their appearance and disappearance with
their mass movement to some other place, though the flocks of
day-flying migrants in spring and autumn could not have escaped
the notice of people living along the migration routes.

> And when her time is come,
> Her voice we no longer hear,
> And where she goes we do not know,
> Until another year.

It was firmly believed that swallows hibernated in the mud of
ponds, not such an absurd assumption when we remember that the
autumn flocks preparing for migration often gather in reed beds.
Cuckoos were said to change into hawks during the winter. And
when the idea that birds might leave a locality became credible
their journeys were imagined as leading them to strange places, as

when the Bishop of Hereford recorded in medieval times his belief that swallows fly to the moon at the end of summer.

The pieces of evidence came together gradually. Although not all his friends were fully convinced, Gilbert White of Selborne believed that he had the evidence for the yearly journeys of birds. Information gleaned by observers in many countries was gradually pooled as international interest grew and the barriers of language broke down, and the observation of migratory birds became a study which drew the ornithologists of the world together. Birds were seen on successive dates at different places, apparently following a route, and methods of marking them were devised so that it could be said with certainty that a given bird had in fact made the journey from one place to another. In this work amateur and professional co-operated most fruitfully, so that in the last fifty years of intensive work ten million or more birds have been marked in Great Britain, America and Germany alone. Not every bird in a flock can be traced, for the task of catching and marking them is too great, and of those that are marked only a small number are seen again. If they are of a species sought for food or sport then the number found again is comparatively great, sometimes as many as a fifth of the ringed birds being recovered. But the rate of recovery of small birds is much lower and usually not more than one out of several hundred marked birds is found again.

These observations of individual birds are backed up by records kept at the bird observatories which have been set up on the migration routes. Here the times and directions of the flocks are noted as they pass overhead or settle for a while. To mention only two of these establishments, there is the famous station on the island of Heligoland, now re-opened, and an almost equally famous station on the Fair Isle between the Orkneys and Shetlands. These island observatories are visited by many birds which alight there on their flight across the sea, small birds particularly being unable to make the long distance crossings, especially in bad weather (plate 8).

More information comes from the army of amateur observers

both on the coasts and inland who note and report the passage of various wild birds, performing as valuable a service as those who watch for migrating butterflies—indeed they are very often the same people. With scraps of information from all these different sources a picture has been built up of the extraordinary journeys of birds, which in the large numbers involved, their regularity and accuracy of navigation are unique among animals.

Many birds make long daily journeys from their nests. This is particularly true of sea-birds which, nesting on the cliffs, may fly far out to sea to find their food. But though their return requires accurate navigation, the distances they fly are not comparable with those flown by some migrating birds. The hunters are flying along coasts which are known to them; they are not striking out over unknown country as many young birds do when they begin their autumn flight. Sometimes birds gather together into breeding colonies for the summer but disperse widely in the winter. Gannets, for example, breed along the west and north coasts of Britain but during the winter they spread widely, being found far south on the Atlantic coasts of Europe and Africa. Like the daily food flights this is a dispersion not a true migration, for the birds spread out in all directions. Nevertheless these flights pose the same problems of navigation as does migration between summer and winter areas.

The term migration has come to be used for the movement of the centre of gravity of a whole population from one place to another, though this may not be a satisfactory definition when applied to insects as we have seen (p. 62). In dispersion individuals may move in quite different directions. Migration in birds is also distinguished as a two-way journey, to the breeding-ground in spring and to the winter quarters in autumn. The routes they follow are not always known in detail, but perhaps they are the same for both journeys. We have seen that the seasonal movements of butterflies appear to fit in with this definition, though their breeding areas are not generally so fixed as those of birds which may nest in the same place year after year.

In the northern hemisphere the movements are usually north

to south in autumn and south to north in spring. Thus the British Isles are the northern breeding station of swallows which winter around the Mediterranean and in Africa as far south as South

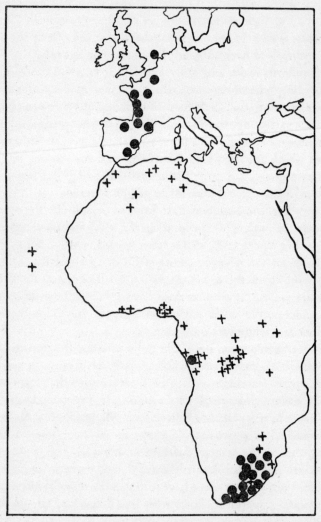

FIG. 34.—Recoveries of swallows banded in Britain and on the Continent. The black circles are those banded in Britain and the crosses those banded on the Continent. (After Landsborough-Thomson.)

Africa itself (fig. 34). We see these birds in the spring and they nest here. On the other hand Britain is the winter quarters for birds such as the fieldfare which breed further north; these winter visitors are here at the southern end of their range and do not nest in this country.

There are many reasons why birds make these long journeys, and they differ from species to species. Temperatures may be more suitable in the breeding area for the young birds, and food supply may be more abundant, which is a very important factor, since the young are voracious and much of their parents' time is spent in collecting food for their offspring. The American house wren, for example, has been found on occasion to feed its young 1,117 times in a day. All this takes time, and as birds usually only feed by day it is not surprising that long daylight hours are a necessity of the breeding areas, and are to be found in the northern spring and early summer.

However, some birds, as Gilbert White noticed, are non-migratory, staying with us all the year round. The robin remains on its territory throughout the winter, a fact which used to be so regularly recorded on the old-style Christmas card. These stay-at-home birds find all that they need in the way of food, nest sites and so forth in one place.

Perhaps in this range of movement, from remaining in the home territory at one extreme, through dispersals, to complete long-distance migration at the other extreme, we can see something of the origin of migration and with it the origin of the bird's power to navigate over long distances. Let us look back to the time when the glaciers were melting after one of the Ice Ages. The temperature was rising and the ice retreating northwards. We can imagine that one population of birds made a spring journey northwards to reach areas which had recently been freed from the ice, finding at the same time cooler and perhaps more favourable temperatures with more hours in which to search for food. On their way they might pass another group which was not migrating (fig. 35). These first movements would only be made by a few birds who in the autumn might wander south again and find their old haunts. These birds were probably more successful in breeding than those that had not moved and, because of their superiority, birds which made the annual journey gradually

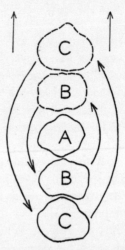

FIG. 35.—Diagram to show a possible origin of the migratory habit in birds. The population A remains sedentary but as the glaciers retreat northwards first B and then C move north and return south again, passing over A.

became established in the stock until at last all of that population joined in the migration. The distances involved would perhaps have been relatively small and would have called for no more than an ability to navigate by recognizable landmarks, but those birds that could navigate would be at an advantage. Later another population still farther south might also begin to fly northward annually but their northern bases could be to the north of the other birds because the ice had retreated farther. Their journeys would be longer. This is all highly speculative and quite unproven, but as we have few direct clues the origin of bird migration is in large part a matter for speculation anyway.

This is not the place to discuss the stimulus which causes birds to migrate. Suffice it to say that length of day, increasing in spring and decreasing in autumn, seems to be a basic influence. It acts in turn through the eyes—which detect the light—the brain, and the

7 Close-up of desert locusts in flight. Note that
they are not all heading in the same direction

8 A migrating flock of oystercatchers on Oldeoog Island, observation station of the Ornithological Research Institute, Vogelwarte Helgoland

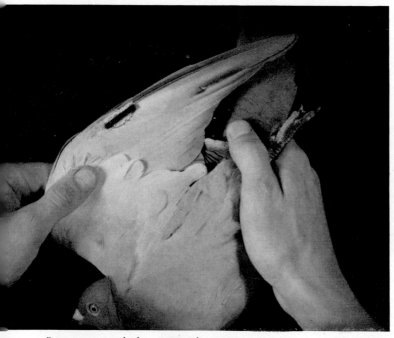

9 Bar magnet attached to a pigeon's wing

ductless glands, particularly the pituitary, which stimulate the increase or decrease in the size of the gonads by the hormones released. Here we see once more the influence of the daylight hours on a bird's life; first they control the length of time for feeding, and here they control the onset of the seasonal migration. In the next chapter we shall see the evidence for yet another function, the control of the inner chronometer which the bird carries.

The role of temperature in the northward movement at least is emphasized by the close correspondence between the spring-time advance of swallows, for example, and the lines of increased temperature. This does not necessarily mean that temperature is having a direct effect, for it may merely be producing favourable conditions by opening buds, for instance, or bringing out insects for food. The ruby-throated humming bird advances at about the same speed as the $35°C$ isotherm, the increase in temperature stimulating the flowers on which it feeds to open. Migrations down mountain sides—shorter, of course, than the long-distance migrations of swallows—are made to avoid the onset of winter cold. The Himalayan redstart, for example, does this, returning up the mountain in spring to escape from the summer heat in the valleys.

Birds may feed on a very restricted diet, choosing one sort of food found in a few places only. The search for this food may produce a migration. Open-billed storks breed on the Zambesi river during the dry season when the mud is exposed and they can feed on the molluscs. They migrate northward to arrive on the upper Nile in the northern dry season where food is once more available, while the Zambesi mud is covered. This is a trans-equatorial journey, and relatively unusual, for most migratory birds live in the northern hemisphere.

Other birds make even longer journeys than this. These carry them almost the greatest distance they can go, that is, from Pole to Pole. Arctic terns are long-distance fliers of this kind. They nest in the Canadian Arctic within a thousand miles of the Pole, and fly southwards across the Atlantic down the west coast of Africa to winter on the pack-ice of the Antarctic (fig. 36). Wilson's petrels journey in the opposite direction, for they breed on the Antarctic islands and fly north for the northern summer, passing up the opposite side of the Atlantic to the tern, following the American coast (fig. 37). They have not been reported as far

FIG. 36.—Diagram of the migratory path of Arctic terns from their northern breeding grounds to their southern wintering places.

north as the Arctic tern's breeding ground, but even then this journey is of at least 7,000 miles without allowing for wandering. This is not hearsay, but well confirmed by observation.

Fig. 37.—Diagram of the migratory path of Wilson's petrel from the breeding grounds in Antarctica to their north Atlantic wintering places. The arrows reach as far north as these birds have been recorded.

One may well wonder at what speeds birds fly when they migrate. We know, for example, that the Wilson's petrels have all left the Antarctic in March or April, and that they have all passed the equator on their northward journey by June. This sort of observation simply gives an idea of the lowest possible speed, but clearly some birds will fly more quickly than this. In one or two cases a marked bird has been recovered miles away soon after being released. This gives a more direct estimate of speed. A mallard had covered 900 miles in five days, a turnstone was found 510 miles away twenty-five hours after being released, and a shearwater covered 3,050 miles in twelve days. There is no doubt that the mallard and the shearwater were not flying continuously, and it is very unlikely that the turnstone had done so. The distances covered are measured along the direct line from place to place, but it is hardly likely that the birds followed the direct route. More probably they wandered extensively. No entirely successful method has been devised of recording how long a bird has been flying and how long resting, but on the whole the average speed of migration based on such observations is 7 to 20 m.p.h. This is lower than the speeds at which birds are known to fly, for song birds seem to have an air speed of between 20 and 37 m.p.h. while ducks fly at 44 to 59 m.p.h. White storks have been paced by an aeroplane flying at 48 m.p.h.

These storks were at 4,200 feet. Migrating birds do not usually travel as high as this, but mostly below 3,000 feet. It is notoriously difficult for a person on the ground to judge accurately the height of something moving through the air, we tend to exaggerate very easily and this no doubt is the origin of the idea that migrating flocks habitually fly at heights greater than those given above. Most birds, particularly the small ones, are usually only at a few hundred feet.

Thus we see the background against which these fantastic journeys take place. But there remains one characteristic which concerns us most of all, the accuracy with which the migrants make their landfalls and find their winter or summer quarters. Despite their long journey swallows will return to the very nest they left the previous autumn. Sometimes the breeding area is very restricted and isolated, yet the birds can still manage to find it, like the bristle-thighed curlew which nests in Alaska but passes the winter 6,000 miles across the Pacific on Tahiti, Hawaii and the neighbouring islands (fig. 38). To make this journey the minimum sea crossing is 2,000 miles without landmarks. It breeds in a limited area of Alaska, but the islands to which it flies in the autumn subtend an arc of about 45 deg. at its breeding place.

Thus great accuracy is required for the return journey to Alaska, which is not necessary when heading southwards in autumn. But even this feat of navigation does not equal that of the great

Fig. 38.—Diagram of the migratory path of the bristle-thighed curlew from its wintering area in east and central Polynesia to its breeding grounds in western Alaska.

shearwater. This bird nests on the islands of the Tristan de Cunha group, a tiny patch in the ocean in the South Atlantic. Yet after nesting the shearwaters range far from the islands over the whole of the Atlantic, reaching as far north as latitude 60 deg. But at each breeding season they return to these islands from all parts of their wide summer range. To make such a landfall very accurate navigation indeed is demanded.

Does there, in fact, seem to be direct evidence of a bird's ability to navigate? Certainly the examples which have been given indicate strongly that the birds involved can and do guide themselves rather than drift in a general direction. In other words they aim for a goal, though we shall not commit ourselves as to whether that goal is sought consciously or unconsciously. Obviously the terms conscious and unconscious based on human

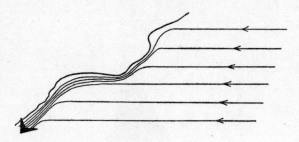

FIG. 39.—Diagram to show how migration on a broad front overland may be deflected and concentrated to follow the coast.

subjective thought can have no meaning in animals, so what we really mean is whether the position is learned or the navigational directions are inherited.

When birds are flying in mass over open country they tend to follow one set direction, often spread out over a wide advancing front of fifteen or more miles, and on occasion even as much as 600 miles. Their course points to their winter or summer quarters as the case may be. However, topographical features may cause the birds to change direction. This is particularly obvious at the coast, for there, or even a few miles inland, land birds leave the main direction in which they have been flying over land to turn and follow the coast line, which may lead them very much off their course. They seem to choose to turn in the direction closest to the one they have been following; for example, the migration of many European birds is sometimes canalized along the south coast of the North Sea (fig. 39). Land birds seem to have an aversion to crossing open sea, which encourages deflection from their course, but this is not the complete explanation, for birds like swallows, flying in from the sea, may turn to follow the coast for at least a short distance. Further, if conditions for migration are at their best the coast line does not divert as many flocks as when conditions are less favourable.

A well-known example of the deflection and indeed almost complete reversal of migrating birds by topographical features is the route of the turkey buzzards passing along the isthmus of

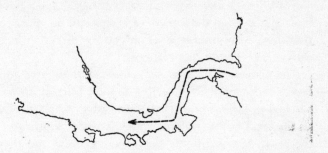

FIG. 40.—The migration route of turkey buzzards along the isthmus of Panama.

Panama. Heading north-westwards at first, they are led south-west or even southwards as they follow the land bridge between the continents; but as they fly over Nicaragua their route once again turns north-westwards (fig. 40). Butterflies also tend to follow natural 'leading lines.'

When darkness falls and the natural features are less visible, migration continues on a broader front, taking up the standard direction followed by that species once again. Land birds then fly out to sea without being affected by the coast over which they fly.

The main migratory direction of most European species of song bird is not strictly due north to south but rather north-east to south-west; thus, starlings come to Britain in the winter from the general area of Norway, Southern Sweden, the Baltic States, Denmark and Holland. But this generalization does not apply to all birds, for the white storks of eastern and north-eastern Europe travel south-eastwards through Palestine and the Sudan to South Africa, though the storks of West Germany go south-westwards in the same direction as the song birds. Perhaps this difference may date from the Ice Age when the ice-cap stretched to the Alps and forced the animals of Europe either south-westwards into the Iberian peninsula or south-eastwards into the Balkans. The isolation of the two populations apparently permitted the evolution of complete differences between many animals, newts, toads and crows among them, so that when they met again after the retreat of the ice they might no longer interbreed freely. Though the storks were isolated no evolutionary change in their body structure took place, the differences arising only in their behaviour, resulting in a difference of migratory direction between the eastern and western populations.

The tendency to migrate in one of these two directions is fixed. It is apparently inherited and not learned, for storks were hatched in Essen from eggs laid in East Prussia and released after all the local storks—which would fly to the south-west—had left the area. Afterwards the birds were tracked and they seem to have kept to their ancestral south-south-easterly direction (fig. 41). We shall look again at this inherited tendency as an explanation of the bird's navigational powers, but for the time being it provides us with evidence of an ability to navigate on a particular bearing and for a definite distance.

Wind does not have the effect on birds that it does on locusts. They are better able to battle with it than the insects. So their flights continue and indeed are more frequent in high winds. Like locusts, birds fly lower in high winds; starlings 'creep' over the countryside when the wind is strong and against them, but travel at 200 to 300 feet when they are helped by a following wind. They can compensate for a change in the wind by altering their heading so that their course remains the same, apparently using the landmarks below them to determine the extent of their drift. It is interesting that the higher fliers seem less able to correct for drift. A possible explanation might be that at a height their movement relative to the landmarks visible at that height is not sufficient to permit them to navigate; if this were so, it would be another parallel to the behaviour of locust swarms. The above-mentioned aversion of land birds to crossing the sea may stem from the absence of landmarks and therefore their inability to correct for drift. We saw how locusts were also unable to navigate when they flew over water.

But migrational navigation is not the only possibility. Birds can

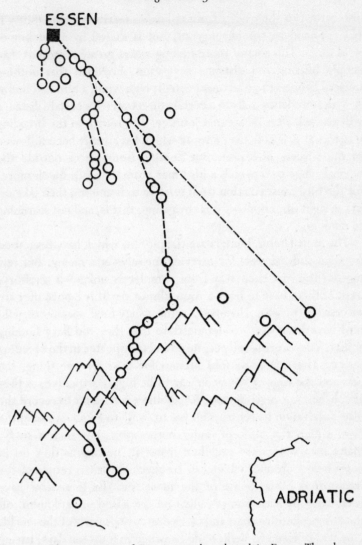

FIG. 41.—The recoveries of Prussian storks released in Essen. The observations of what were probably the same parties are joined by broken lines. Note that they tended to maintain the south-south-easterly direction which they would in their normal areas, though the Alps appear to have deflected some. (After Schüz.)

also return to their nests from unknown territory. This ability is not confined to homing pigeons, but is shared by a number of wild birds. This sort of route-finding makes greater demands than simple bearing and distance navigation. Provided that nothing unusual happens, like an unexpectedly high wind, a bird hatched at A with a tendency to fly in a certain direction for a certain distance will reach B after its autumn journey. The return to the breeding quarters at A is now over a route which has already been followed in the reverse direction. But homing from places outside the normal range over which a bird may roam demands much more, for the bird must position itself relative to home and then take off in the right direction—if it is navigating, that is, and not searching at random.

The most famous homers are the pigeons which have been used for thousands of years for carrying messages and racing. But few pigeons can find their way from completely unknown territory, most of them have to learn a route almost slavishly before they are successful (p. 93). However, some thirty-four species of wild bird have been used to demonstrate that they too have homing ability. They were usually captured and transported in the breeding season. There were various reasons for this: for one thing, the nest and the eggs or young appear to be highly attractive, as they are to homing pigeons, too; for another, it is easier to record the bird's arrival on its return, if it has to come to a known place, the nest, which can be kept under observation. For such a study, Manx shearwaters are excellent material, nesting as they do in holes below ground, which can be checked for the return of the transported birds. Some of the most remarkable returns have been made by shearwaters caught on the island of Skokholm, off the Pembrokeshire coast and carried to various parts of the world. One was released in Venice and returned in fourteen days, having covered a distance which would have been 930 miles if it had flown directly over land or 3,700 miles if it followed the Mediterranean sea coast to the Atlantic and so to Wales (fig. 42). But this bird was surpassed by another which set up what must be a record for homing. This bird was despatched by Dr. Matthews of Cambridge University to Boston, U.S.A., where it was released on his behalf. It arrived back on Skokholm twelve and a half days later, beating by almost half a day the letter informing him of its

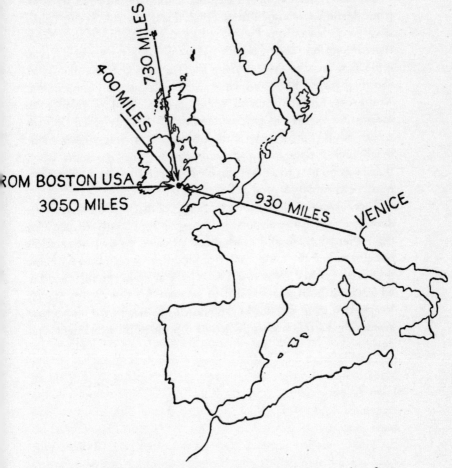

FIG. 42.—Examples of the distances covered by shearwaters taken from Skokholm on their return to the island.

release. Now it is very unlikely that either shearwater had been to the release points in their wandering life, for both lie well outside the normal range of British shearwaters; they could not therefore have had previous knowledge of the route. Moreover, the journey from America took place mainly over the sea, as featureless to a bird, probably, as it is to most human beings.

But other smaller birds can home also. Swallows and starlings from Berlin have homed from London and Madrid, Polish storks have come back from Lydda in Palestine (admittedly this is on their migration route), noddy and sooty terns transported 1,300 miles flew back to their nests in the Tortugas and an alpine swift returned from Lisbon covering 1,000 miles in sixty-nine hours. Not every bird of each of these species could perform such spectacular flights; in fact, a number of those released did not return at all. But in general the proportion of returns was high, much higher than in experiments carried out in winter when there was no nest to attract the bird back and 10 per cent returns must be considered good.

There seems no doubt then that birds of many species have well developed navigational powers, being able not only to perform the rather more simple bearing and distance type of orientation but also to find their way back from territory which they have not previously visited. We must now look at some of the theories which have been put forward to account for this facility which has puzzled man, envious in the knowledge of his own blundering around the earth's surface, when he is unaided by instruments and devices.

CHAPTER VII

Aerial Navigators

T HERE can be no denying that year after year birds travel long distances between their winter and summer quarters which are in roughly the same places every year. How can they do this? And what seems more puzzling, how can the young birds hatched in the north find their way south to their winter quarters without the help of their parents, undertaking a journey they have never made before? The young birds often leave before the older ones and therefore get no guidance from the more experienced navigators. Moreover, birds can find their way home over unfamiliar territory, as the shearwaters did on their return to Skokholm from Venice and Boston.

We can at least get some indications of how a bird navigates when we study homing pigeons, something which pigeon fanciers have been doing for years. But we must be careful not to expect to get from the pigeon the explanation for all homing by all species. The rock doves of the east, from which the homing pigeon has been bred, do not migrate, but stay in one neighbourhood for most of their life. Yet each year swallows, and hundreds of other species of birds, make their two journeys. They are the true travellers and it is in their navigational powers that the greatest mystery lies.

Any fancier will tell you that it is rare to get a pigeon which can home from a long distance at the first trial. And as people differ in their intelligence, so individual pigeons differ in their ability to home. The training of a racer consists of taking it a short distance away from its loft and releasing it to fly back, then taking it farther and farther as its training proceeds. The bird is always taken in the same direction and gradually learns more and more about returning to its loft over a certain strip of country. But take a trained pigeon in a different direction and it may be lost.

Pigeons are easily bred and carried about and it is not surprising that investigations on these birds have influenced ideas about how wild birds navigate on their seasonal journeys. A great deal is known about pigeon navigation, but by no means everything.

One way of approaching any problem of this kind is to speculate how a human being would cope with the same situation and then to devise experiments to test whether the birds do what a human might do. For example, it might be that pigeons learn a route by seeing and memorizing landmarks just as we do. These would have to be visible from the height at which a pigeon flies, i.e. about 300 feet, and certainly not more than 3,000 feet. Now suppose it had learned the landmarks around its home loft. If it could see these then it could fly towards them; in the same way it could fly to familiar objects which it had learned to recognize *en route* back to the loft. This idea gets some support from the way in which bad weather and particularly fog causes many pigeons to get lost.

Unfortunately for this theory, however, the distances to which a pigeon is taken towards the end of its training are much greater than the earlier ones and may be as much as 100 to 150 miles. Knowing the height from which a pigeon sees the countryside, it is a simple calculation to prove that its horizon would not extend far enough to include the country flown over on previous training runs, so that we should not expect a pigeon just released and climbing to its flying height to be able to see familiar places, though, of course, in the earlier and shorter training distances it probably could do. There is little doubt that knowledge of the landmarks is in fact very important in aiding a pigeon to find its way and many individual birds may have no other method of navigation, but it seems to function only over fairly short distances. On the other hand, some pigeons can home from totally unfamiliar territory. The explanation must lie elsewhere than in an ability to learn to recognize landmarks.

Can it be that the pigeons remember the twists and turns of the journey as they are carried to their release point? It is a little hard to imagine how they can do so, cooped up in a basket pushed from guard's van to platform, sometimes in the light of

Fig. 43.—Sketch plan of the Hampton Court Maze.

day, sometimes in the darkness of a railway truck. But it is a possibility. If you enter Hampton Court Maze (fig. 43) and you turn to the left, provided that you then turn to the right twice and to the left three times when you have to make a choice, you reach the centre. To get out again you only have to remember the turns you have made as you walked in and reverse them. But the chance that this is how a bird navigates can be eliminated without much difficulty, for sparrows and pigeons, among other birds, have been transported in cages which revolved all the time and often unevenly, so that the birds should have been thoroughly disorganized. Dr. Matthews reports that some of his pigeons went to sleep as he transported them, so that it is very unlikely that they were consciously noting the turns and twists of the car in which they were travelling. The birds from the revolving cages did no worse in homing than the birds which had had a smooth passage.

There are a number of ways in which familiar territory could be reached from a point in the unknown without navigating directly towards it. Let us assume that a number of birds fly in all directions outwards from a release point. Some of them will be heading in the right direction, and if only they fly long enough they will reach some place they know, and a few more will pass near enough to the home area to see it and turn aside from their track to reach it (fig. 44). An approximate calculation can be made of the number of birds likely to home if we know how far away the release point is from familiar territory and also the size of that territory, as the diagram shows. Unfortunately this does

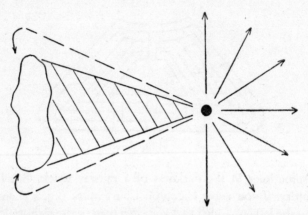

Fig. 44.—Radial search. Those birds taking up any heading in the shaded sector will reach familiar territory while those within the broken lines will pass so close that they will see it and turn aside. The other birds would be lost.

not usually fit in with the number of birds which actually do return successfully. According to theory a larger and larger proportion of the birds released should get lost the farther away the release point is from known territory of fixed size, but it is not always so. It seems we must abandon this explanation too and seek for one which would give every bird an equal chance of getting home.

Let us suppose that a bird flies in an ever-widening spiral after it has been released. As it flies it searches the ground for familiar things, valleys, houses, towns. So that the search may be complete and efficient, scanning the whole countryside, the gyres of the spiral must not be further apart than twice the distance the bird can see to the side, otherwise there will be parts of the landscape it misses (fig. 45). Now the farther away from home the bird starts the distance it has to fly will be disproportionately greater, for the distance along the spiral increases far more than the

10 Kramer's device for studying the orientation abilities of birds. (*a*) The screen so arranged that a bird in the cage within sees nothing apart from the attendant and the sky. (*b*) A starling within the cage around which are spaced feeding boxes to which it is trained to go

11　Salmon　jumping
Brooks　Falls,　Alaska

increase in direct distance, therefore the time it takes will be very much greater than if it had flown straight back. But the relationship between the length of the flight and the time actually

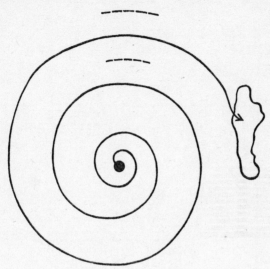

Fig. 45.—Spiral search. The broken lines indicate the supposed width of the bird's field of vision.

taken does not indicate that birds have flown on a spiral course. Anyway, neither of these hypotheses is satisfactory for the good reason that when pigeons are released, after circling once or twice, they fly in roughly the correct direction. Starlings released in unknown territory do the same (fig. 46.) Only in a few instances have the tracks of birds on release been like the beginning of a spiral, in so few cases in fact that it might be sheer chance that they did so. Nevertheless, no bird has ever been followed the whole way back, and we can only conjecture what they do from the few clues we have.

A bird's main sense organs are its eyes and their main sense is, therefore, vision. Their other senses, apart from hearing, are not so well developed; for example, they are very insensitive to smells, so useful to many other animals in finding their way. This makes it likely that an explanation of their homing ability will involve their visual sense. Many migrating birds follow the lines of natural features, river valleys or sea coasts, for example, but this may have another explanation in that many birds that follow

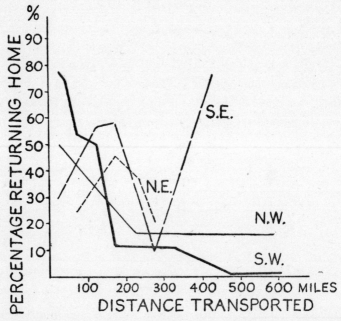

FIG. 46.—The proportion of starlings returning successfully after being transported various distances. The figures are arranged according to the compass direction in which the birds were taken. The direction does not seem to affect homing and the ability to return does not always decrease with increase in distance. (After Matthews.)

the coasts feed on the shores and at river mouths. The valleys are probably more hospitable than the open plains or the hills. They fly where their food is. Mountains are not barriers, at least to swallows, so the indirect route along the valleys may be followed for some other reason, not concerned with navigation. But some birds do seem to be able to appreciate features in the landscape which would give an indication of direction: rivers which will lead downstream to the sea, or differences between north and south slopes of a hill, for example. Gannets released well inland on heath country over which it is most unlikely that they had ever flown before turned towards the sea after a short reconnaissance as if they could perceive indications from the lie of the landscape which enabled them to take the correct heading.

The problem has thus become a mystery, for it appears that none of the aspects of the senses with which we are familiar can be invoked to supply an answer. We must therefore turn to possibilities outside our own sensory range and particularly to those natural phenomena which we use for navigation with the help of instruments. The earth has two magnetic poles and spread between them are lines of magnetic force by which we can navigate with the aid of mechanical devices to detect the earth's magnetism. A compass needle turns to the north but that alone does not tell us where we are, merely which way we are facing. The lines of force run in one direction and to plot our position we need another set of lines representing some other measurable quantity which cross the lines of force. These are supplied by the lines of equal declination or dip. Now to find our position on this grid we need two co-ordinates, the direction of our compass needle and the amount of the declination. Can we expect a bird to be able to measure these? It seems unlikely, since we ourselves can only do it with the aid of complicated apparatus. This grid is moreover unsatisfactory, for at certain places on the earth's surface the lines of equal deviation and dip are parallel.

But what are we to say, then, of the reports of migrating birds and particularly homing pigeons thrown off course and thoroughly confused by wireless stations, apparently by the electrical disturbances during transmission? The numbers of times this has been reported is small compared with the probable number of times birds have flown close to transmitters and been undisturbed (and therefore not reported!). Also the reports have not proved beyond doubt that it was wireless waves that caused the confusion. Indeed shrike could not be trained to respond to high-frequency radiation of any intensity, provided that the wave was continuous. However, when pulsed waves were used birds did respond but this may have been due to the effect of such waves on the bird's body rather than due to the upsetting of the working of a sense organ, for waves of this sort produce all sorts of physical effects on the tissues. Pigeons have been carefully observed in radar beams and are apparently unruffled by the waves which are bombarding them. These are artificial stimuli stronger than the natural ones. Evidence of the lack of effect of the earth's magnetic field can be got by attaching magnetized bars to the wings of one set of birds (plate 9) and unmagnetized bars of the same weight and size to others and then observing what effect these have on their ability to navigate. The bars are magnetized sufficiently strongly to counteract the magnetic field of the earth. In no case have the birds with magnets been less able to navigate than the birds with unmagnetized bars. This seems to dispose of the theory of navigation by terrestrial magnetism.

There are other physical forces acting on bodies flying over, or travelling on, the earth. One of these is Corioli's force. This is a force whose strength is expressed as the product of a number of factors resulting from the earth's rotation. It acts when a body accelerates relatively to the surface of the earth. The force acting on a body is the sum of its speed and the centrifugal force of the earth but with an extra amount added, Corioli's force. It will cause movement of the fluid in a small ring-shaped, fluid-filled tube which is moved relatively to the axis of the earth. The force moving the liquid depends on the size of the ring. Now this sounds very far from having anything to do with a migrating bird but in fact in the bird's inner ear lie the semicircular canals (fig. 47) responsible for the perception of acceleration; they exist in human ears, too. Each of these canals is a ring filled with fluid, and in each ring is a small patch of sensitive hairs which are bent by any movement of the liquid. These hairs are connected to nerve cells and their movement is registered in the brain. Now the connection is clear, for here is apparently the ideal organ for perceiving this force. Admittedly the bird would have to swing its head to impose the necessary relative movement on the ring but that does not seem impossible, for it would not have to wag its head continuously but only very occasionally to find its position. However there is what appears at the moment to be an insurmountable difficulty, for the amount of the force which would act on a ring as small as the tiny canal in the ear of a song

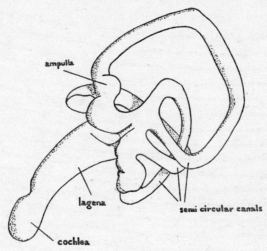

ampulla

lagena

semi circular canals

cochlea

FIG. 47.—The inner ear of a bird.

bird has been shown to be smaller than the force to which tiny particles are submitted, called Brownian movement. In other words the molecules of the liquid in the canal will be moving about with a force great enough to mask any effect Corioli's force might have. Therefore it is unlikely that the sensitive hairs could detect the action of this force. Other physical effects of the earth's rotation can be similarly discounted. These possibilities do not seem to be worth considering further; but we have only dismissed them on theoretical grounds, for we have no direct proof that birds cannot perceive them. It is merely highly unlikely.

We have said that the the problem of bi-co-ordinate navigation is to find the two systems which will form a satisfactory grid. It would be possible to invoke Corioli's force and combine it with the lines of equal magnetic intensity. However, this grid is not altogether suitable, for in places the lines of equal intensity of the two forces cross at acute angles or even run parallel to each other (fig. 48). But the use of this grid has been put to the test in America. First pigeons were tested to see whether magnets

FIG. 48.—Grid of Corioli's force (thick lines) and equal magnetic vertical force over part of North America.

upset their homing; the results were unconvincing, which is not surprising in view of the number of later tests which have been negative.

The crucial test would be to see what happens when the birds' normal choice of reference on the grid is confused. It has been pointed out that the grid is not a perfect one, since in one part of America there are two points which have identical co-ordinates (fig. 48). The test would be to take birds from a loft kept at one of these points and release them between the two to see whether any of them flew to the second point instead of returning to home. This was tried, but the birds showed no tendency to go wrong. Thus a practical test has not shown that pigeons are able to appreciate the grid of magnetic force and Corioli's force. We must continue the search, sift and if necessary eliminate other possible factors.

The routes of migratory birds are unvarying year after year. But the way in which they follow the routes differs with the species. Storks fly individually, starlings in flocks; sometimes the young leave first, sometimes the older birds; and sometimes the bands are mixed, with the older birds apparently leading—family groups of geese, for example, seem to be organized in this way. The permanency of the routes does suggest that there may be an inherited sense of direction, or at least an inherited tendency to fly in a particular direction, two rather different things. It is very easy to suggest this for it seems to answer all our difficulties; it is even easy to demonstrate it, but it must not be forgotten that even if the direction is inherited, to maintain any direction at all, the bird has to navigate and use some sort of guide.

When young birds which are migrating or are just about to fly off on their autumn or spring journey are moved away from the usual thoroughfare of their flight, they are often recaptured at places which indicate that they were following a direction parallel to their real route. Young crows were caught in Alberta in the summer and kept in cages until the adults had left the area on their flight southwards to their winter quarters, which were to the south-east in Kansas and Oklahoma 1,500 miles away.

These young birds had never made this journey, for they had hatched in the spring of that year. They were taken away from the places where they had been trapped so that they should not be

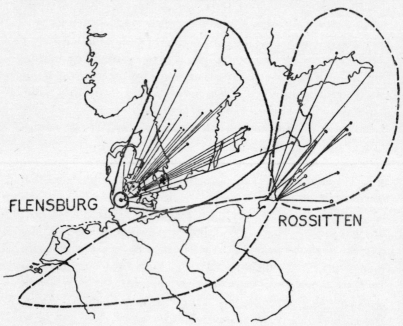

FLENSBURG

ROSSITTEN

FIG. 49.—Recoveries of starlings released at Flensburg after being transported from Rossitten. The broken lines indicate the normal distribution of the starlings and within it can be seen the recoveries of the control birds which were permitted to fly on from Rossitten. Note that one bird flew over into the normal range. (After Ruppell.)

able to recognize any familiar landmarks, then they were released. Fortunately over half of the birds were found again and most of them had flown off far enough to be considered as having begun to migrate. All of these had set off in the general direction of their winter quarters. So it seems that even without the guidance of older birds that knew the route, the young birds could at least find the right general direction.

But experience of migrating does seem to help, perhaps by transforming the rather general knowledge of the young birds

into the more accurate navigation of the older ones. Hooded
crows on the western shores of the Baltic and in North Germany
migrate in spring to breed in Lithuania, Latvia and Finland. This

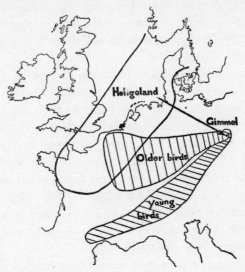

FIG. 50.—Sparrowhawks transported from Heligoland to Gimmel were found
later in the areas shown. The usual area over which the birds are found is
unshaded.

north-westerly direction is typical of many Continental birds—
they return in a south-westerly direction in the autumn; 900 of
the crows, mainly inexperienced birds born the previous year and
therefore knowing the south-westerly journey only, were captured
in the Rossitten area and released at Flensburg to the north of
their usual line of migration. Afterwards many were found in
southern Sweden and north-eastern Denmark, so that they must
have flown roughly parallel to their customary route (fig. 49).
They continued to fly back and forth over this path, though a few
birds did find their old breeding places and joined the flocks
there. These were older birds caught by mistake. Their greater
experience seems to have permitted them to make the adjustment.

A similar experiment was done on sparrowhawks, which migrate through Heligoland in autumn south-westwards to their

winter quarters in Holland, Belgium and northern France, some of them coming to south-east England as well. Both young and old birds were captured at Heligoland, taken to the mainland and released at Gimmel in eastern Germany. The young birds seem to have kept to the direction they were going, flying off parallel to their migration course, but many of the older birds regained their old course (fig. 50).

Of course it may be objected that the birds were not showing an inherited sense of direction but had joined local bands of birds and had been swept along with them in their migration. The desire to follow the 'locals' on their flight is very strong; even relatively non-migratory birds may be drawn in. For example, English mallard reared in Finland migrated with the local ducks and returned to the place where they had hatched, not back to England where the eggs had been laid, so they were not forced by some inherited piece of behaviour to go back to a particular place but only to the place from which they had come and which they had learned to recognize as home.

This criticism was answered when young hooded crows were taken to Frankfurt in western Germany and released. In this area there were no local migrating crows for them to follow, yet they flew north-eastwards, the correct direction for their spring migration.

Crows migrate by day and it therefore seems possible that they fly in a particular direction with respect to the sun. In fact there is now increasing evidence that the sun is probably the most important guide for a migrating bird, and for a homing pigeon for that matter. Perhaps this might be expected, for birds do not migrate in fog nor in bad weather, in other words, at times when the sun will not be plain to see, though many do travel at night when direction finding probably requires a separate explanation. The first task was to see whether migrating birds could be tricked by altering the position of the sun or by hiding it from them. Obviously this would be almost impossible with birds flying high in the air but it had been noticed that warblers, shrikes and starlings, among other birds, make what are called

intention movements at the time of migration. Whether in cages
or in the open, they sit on the perches pointing their heads in the
direction in which they are going to migrate, fluttering their
wings or even making short flights in that direction and returning

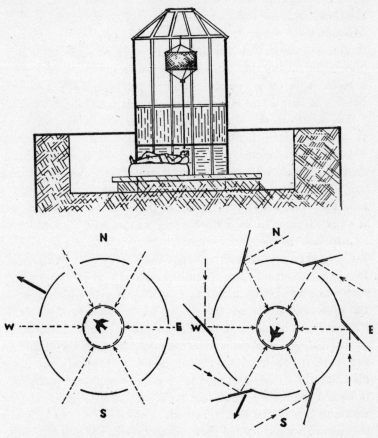

F<small>IG</small>. 51.—Above, diagram of Kramer's method of observing birds in the small
cage suspended within a glass-sided enclosure.
Below, two examples of the results obtained. Left, the sun's rays entered
uninterruptedly and the birds flew in a north-westerly direction. Right,
shutters bearing mirrors were put up so that the sun's rays were deflected
through 90 deg., the bird's direction changed through almost 90 deg.
also. (After Kramer.)

to their perches. Dr. Kramer in Germany constructed cages beneath the floor of which he could lie and looking upwards see the direction in which the birds were pointing. He found that they would only do this when they could see the sun or the sky close to it. One cage was fitted with six square windows through which the birds could see only patches of sky slightly above the horizon. Mirrors were then arranged outside the windows so that the direction from which the light came was changed by a right angle. The bird in this cage turned and faced to the south-west at a right angle to its original heading and steadfastly kept this heading as long as the mirrors were in that position (fig. 51).

The sequel to this was that Kramer was able to train starlings to take food from a particular box set in a particular compass direction from the centre of the cage with six windows (plate 10). And more, the bird could pick out the right box at any time of the day, so that it must have been able to compensate for the sun's movement and not merely have been going to the box which was at a certain angle to the sun wherever the sun was. If a bird learns to associate the place in which a box stands with the position of the sun, this suggests that it might use the sun as a guide when flying. As a matter of fact, it almost seemed that for the starlings such a task was easier than always picking the box which stood in the direction of the sun which the birds found hard to learn. Pigeons were not quite so good at learning to do this, but this is an interesting comparison with the complete inability of finches and starlings to learn to choose boxes in particular compass directions in a room arranged to give them no directional clues. In such a room they would not have a guide such as the sun by which to 'place' the box and so could not discriminate between the boxes arranged around them unless they had an absolute sense of direction. In fact a starling inside a tent where it was shielded from clues and outside of which was put up an artificial sun could learn to go to the right box. If the artificial sun was put in a position similar to that occupied by the sun at that particular time of day the correct box was visited, but if it was moved to some other position in the artificial sky, another box would be visited, the 'correct' one, however, with respect to the 'sun's' false position (fig. 52).

As a result of his investigations on pigeons, Dr. Matthews has

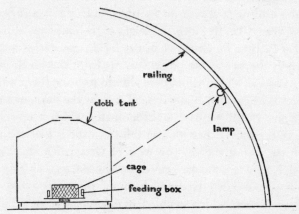

FIG. 52.—Apparatus used to test the influence of the sun on a bird's learning of the position of feeding boxes. The lamp can be moved along the rail giving a 'sun' at different heights which will be seen as a blur within the cage inside the cloth tent. The feeding boxes are arranged round the cage as they are in Plate 10. (After Kramer.)

suggested how a bird might use the sun to recognize its position when it is put down in unknown territory. To the south of its home the sun at its zenith will be higher in the sky, and to the north lower than in its home territory. If, therefore, it can see this difference in height, then it can tell whether it is to the north or south of its home. Now it will not always be flying off when the sun is at its highest, and Matthews suggests that a pigeon can observe the movement of the sun through a small arc, which it can then extend, as it were, in its mind's eye, to the zenith. Then it can know whether the sun is higher or lower than it is at home. The difficulty here is that pigeons fly off and take a direction a very short time after their release, the sun's movement will therefore be very small and the length of the arc it covers short. The smaller the arc the greater the possible error in extending it to the zenith. However, he has pointed out that judgment of moving prey's future position from its movement when first seen is very highly developed in many birds, and this is akin to the extrapolation of the arc of the sun's movement.

But the bird must also know its position to the west or east of its home, the goal of its journey. Height of the sun at any particular time, that is, time by Greenwich, not local time, varies so that it is lower in the sky as we go westwards from the meridian and higher going eastwards. Clocks are altered to bring them into line with local time, so that at any time of the day the sun stands at the same height. But if we have a chronometer which keeps Greenwich time accurately then we can tell from the height of the sun how far we are to the east or west of Greenwich. In place of Greenwich time any standard time can be used, so that if a bird—which does not keep Greenwich time, of course—had some timing mechanism which enabled it to use its home time as a reference, it can compare the height of the sun in this new place—again in its mind's eye—with the sun's position at home at the same time of the day. If the sun was ahead of the 'home' sun the pigeon must be to the east of home, and if behind, that is lower than it would be at home, then it is to the west (fig. 53).

This internal clock would have to be something which the pigeon carried with it, not some natural phenomenon which happened in the world around it. And the mechanism would have to be unaffected by anything happening outside the pigeon's body. Some sort of internal chronometer of this kind is not so impossible as it sounds. There are a number of regular processes going on in a bird's body, or ours, for that matter; our hearts beat, our intestines contract and so forth. Since birds like ourselves have a regulated body temperature, being warm blooded, these activities of their insides are unaffected or relatively unaffected by changes in temperature outside the body; they are insulated from the environment. A hypnotist can suggest to a man under his influence that in, say, 240 minutes, he shall do some action. And indeed, after 240 minutes the man will do it, and there is even some evidence that he does it without seeing a clock. He apparently uses some internal timing mechanism, by which he unconsciously decides that the time is come.

However, it looks very much as though the pigeon's clock is

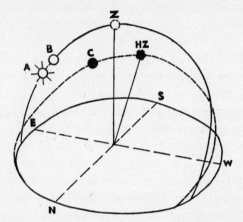

Fig. 53.—Diagram to illustrate the principle of sun-navigation. The sun's actual position is A, the bird observes its movement to B and extrapolates the arc to Z, the sun's zenith at that place. However, in the bird's home territory the sun would be at C at the same time of the day and the zenith at home is HZ. It is therefore south and west of its home.

regulated by the rhythm of day and night which it normally experiences. When pigeons were kept in darkness with irregular periods of artificial light and then subjected to regular artificial 'days' and 'nights' but with 'dawn' coming either before or after dawn outside, their ability to home was upset. According to the sun navigation idea we would expect that a pigeon whose clock was 'fast' would imagine itself to the west of its home when it was released and would fly eastwards, and similarly when its clock was 'slow' it would fly westwards. This, in fact, is what appeared to happen.

The snag seems to be the short time that some birds need to observe the sun, make the necessary 'calculations,' unconscious though they undoubtedly are, and set course for home. Some results suggest that a very short time will suffice. Even when pigeons were only permitted to see the sun for ten seconds, that is, not at all until they were released, their heading after ten seconds' flying was approximately that of their home. However, for various reasons this may be misleading, and very possibly pigeons take much longer to choose their homeward direction, which would be more compatible with the sun-navigation hypothesis.

Thus this method of bi-co-ordinate navigation, using the sun combined with an internal chronometer is not by any means impossible, though one might not expect its accuracy to be as great as the accuracy of a pigeon homing. But perhaps it is not necessary for a bird to home precisely; provided it reaches the general area of its home it can, like an ant, search about for its nest or loft.

Night-flying birds can apparently remember a direction which they took up by the sun just before it set. But garden warblers and blackcaps can navigate without previously seeing the sun. Indeed they can do so even if they have been reared out of sight of the sky. On the first occasion on which they are allowed to see the night sky they take up the direction in which their species always migrates at that time. Cloud confuses them, and bright moonlight causes them to fly towards the moon. Ideal conditions seem to be a clear moonless night when the stars are not shining too brightly. Their knowledge of the constellations, if, indeed, this is the means by which they navigate, is apparently inborn.

This new factor makes bird navigation even more remarkable, and shows vividly how much remains to be discovered. It is most unlikely that any one explanation will be found which will apply to all birds at all times, especially since so many birds migrate at night. A combination of stimuli, probably all of them visual ones, may well be found to act together, each playing its role at appropriate moments.

CHAPTER VIII

Water Ways

E ACH spring and autumn the watchers on the migration routes see great columns of birds streaming across the sky on their journeys to and from their breeding places. They can be caught and counted, tagged and traced, so that their routes can be mapped and the history of the travellers revealed. But how frequently are shoals of fish seen on the move? In the main the great numbers of fish which must move about together give no sign on the surface of their progress. We know that some fish appear in one area at a particular time of the year to disappear a little later, leaving the fishermen to haul empty nets. But these journeys take place away from the sight of man in the open sea, often at fairly deep levels. Indeed the long sea journeys of the eel were only discovered in this century, and complete information is lacking about many common food fish. All we know is where they can be fished at different times. A number of ways of marking fish have been devised so that they can be recognized again; fins may be cut off or special tags attached to them, and the number of recaptures of the marked fish is large enough to give a fair indication of where the fish have come from. But unlike birds they cannot be watched as they journey from the place in which they were marked to the place where they are recaptured.

Since it is of economic importance to know everything we can about the life histories of the fish we eat, work has been concentrated on these. For example, we know something of the movements of cod. Like many fish, mature cod seek warmer water, moving in from all parts of the North Sea to the area north and west of the Dogger bank, the fishing areas of Flamborough, Forties, Great Fisher Bank and the Ling Banks (fig. 54). Here they spawn during February, March and April, spreading away from this area to feed all over the North Sea

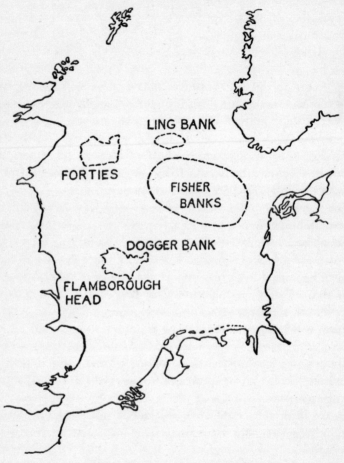

FIG. 54.—The main spawning areas of North Sea cod.

after depositing the infinite millions of eggs they leave there. These eggs drift in the surface waters, hatching soon after being laid, but the fry drift on for some two months before they sink to the bottom to spend the rest of their lives away from the surface. By this time they are to the south and east of the Dogger Bank and, until they are mature at about four years old, they move to either end of the Dogger until they join the coastwards migration to take part in their first spawning.

The North Sea population is apparently separate from that around Iceland, and from the other economically important population of the Barents Sea and Spitsbergen areas. From these last two areas the mature fish also swim to warmer waters near a coast, the former to the south and west of Iceland, the latter among and around the islands off the north-west Norwegian coast.

As the fishing season advances the herring fleets move down the east coast of Britain, followed on land by the fisher lasses who gut and salt the herring. This looks like a human migration following that of the fish, but in fact it is not. The herring of the East Coast are broken up into local races occupying different areas. The fish move inshore to spawn just as the cod do, but the most northerly races do this first, to be followed a week or so later by those to the south and so on in turn. A wave of movement spreads down the coast as the shoals of each race move inshore. Thus their migrations are short, moving roughly due west, not the long direct journey from the north of Scotland down to the Thames estuary, which they appear to be. As each population moves in the fleets move south to fish them.

But much longer journeys are made by other fish. Tunny, for example, breed in the Mediterranean and in the east Atlantic in April and May. Afterwards the schools swim northwards, past the western end of the Channel, up the west coast of Britain, round the northern tip of Scotland and into the North Sea, where they spread southwards, arriving at the Dogger Bank as late as July (fig. 55). The journey from Gibraltar seems to be covered in six to eight weeks. After spending the summer in the North Sea, remaining in the more northern part of it, the tunny turn and swim back the way they came to the breeding areas in the south. This is a long journey and is performed each year, just as migrating birds journey back and forth between

Fig, 55.—The migration of tunny after breeding.

their summer and winter quarters. Moreover, the older tunny seem to arrive at the Norwegian coast before the younger fish. This difference in timing according to age is found in some birds; the young birds who have never flown over the route apparently make slower progress, probably not because they fly more slowly than the older birds but because they wander more.

In one important respect among many others, the likeness between some migrating fish and birds breaks down. A bird spends its young life in the surroundings to which it will return as an adult, but the egg and the fry of a fish like a cod drift away from the spawning area so that the young fish has no chance to learn the characteristics of the breeding places. There must be other factors which draw it back again when it is mature.

The breeding area is usually at the end of the migration route, though some birds do fly on northwards after they have laid their eggs, for example the guillemots on Heligoland. Anchovy do the same. Inhabiting the shallower waters off north-west France and south-west England, they move through the Channel into the North Sea to spawn along its southern coasts, particularly in the estuaries of the Weser, the Elbe and the Scheldt. This has been so only since the final draining of the Zuyder Zee, which was their main spawning place. After egg-laying they continue migrating, swimming out into the North Sea, northwards along the Norwegian coast and the Scottish east coasts. Though many return directly south, some round the North Cape before going to their winter quarters on the continental shelf. We know of this journey because of the records of capture of fish and we piece together what must have happened between.

There seems to be a fairly general rule that fishes on their way to breed move against the current, and after spawning swim with the current, which may also carry the eggs and fry as it does with young cod. The movements of cod fit this rule, but it is best illustrated by observation of plaice. Those plaice that live in the waters off the east coast of Scotland move northwards from as far south as the Firth of Forth to an area in the Moray Firth where they spawn. Along this east coast there is a current travelling in a southerly direction against which the fish must swim to go north. There is another population of plaice in the inshore waters around the Shetland Isles; here the water circulates round the islands in a clockwise direction, against which the spawning fish move northwards along the coast. When fish were transplanted from the east Scotland area to the Shetlands, they made no attempt to swim south, that is with the Shetlands inshore current, to their old spawning grounds, but turned north with the local fish apparently under the influence of the current.

Considerable study has been devoted to finding out how fish can perceive currents. If a fish is moving with the current it will not be able to feel it, for it will, as it were, be part of the body of water which is moving, just as a bird or an insect flying in an even air current is unable to feel in which direction the air is blowing. There will be no pressure differences over a fish's body due to the current, except that there will be of course an increased pressure on its head if it is moving forward, regardless of the direction in which it is travelling in relation to the current. Only when the fish is being passively carried will this pressure be absent. But since it is the same for all the fish's positions it is useless as a means of detecting the direction of the current. We saw that though similar arguments applied to insects, water currents are more homogeneous than air currents and so we cannot suppose that fish can detect the direction of the current directly.

There is, however, one situation in which pressure differences might be utilized; this is when a fish is close to the bottom of a stream. The water moving over a stream bottom, or along its sides for that matter, is travelling more slowly than the water a few inches above the bed, so that a fish turned across the current at an angle would be subject to a greater force on its upper parts than its lower (fig. 56). This would tend to tip the fish over and the tendency would only be eliminated if the fish turned parallel to the current to face either up or down stream. The tendency to tip could be perceived by the inner ear, or by the muscular effort required to keep upright. But though this is mechanically and physiologically possible there is no reason to believe that fish actually do react in this way.

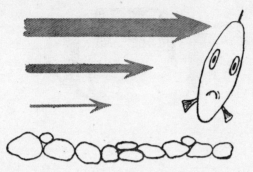

Fig. 56.—Diagram to illustrate how a fish close to the bed of a stream will come under the influence of differences in the speed of the water close to the bed. Thickness of arrows roughly proportional to the speed and force of the water.

We are certain of one mechanism by which a fish can detect a current. It can do this indirectly by perceiving its drift in a similar manner to the way in which a flying locust does. It tends to swim so that the objects which it can see, the weeds and the pebbles on the bottom, for example, are not apparently moving past it. If they appear to move from the back to the front of its eye it is being carried backwards downstream, so it swims hard until it is stationary by the weeds, moving upstream at a speed equal to that of the current which is tending to sweep it backwards. If the current slackens, the images of the weeds will start to move from the front to the back of the fish's eye as it moves forward upstream. So it swims less strongly and preserves its position. All this can be most vividly demonstrated in a simple experiment with sticklebacks. If a stickleback is put into a jam jar full of water standing on a turntable, it will swim vigorously in the opposite direction to that in which the jar is turning provided that the speed is not too great. Place a white screen round the jar so that it can no longer see any landmarks and it will cease to swim forward (fig. 57). Or stop the turntable but arrange to revolve a white screen painted with vertical black stripes round the stationary jar, and the fish will swim in the same direction as the stripes are moving in order to keep its

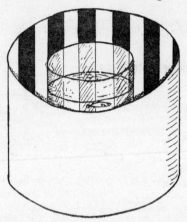

Fig. 57.—The jar containing the stickleback can be rotated or the striped cylinder can be revolved round the stationary jar.

position with them though there is now no current in the water. It is plain that the stickleback is not perceiving the current directly but detects its own motion relative to the background.

It is almost certain that salmon find their way up rivers by using their ability to distinguish the direction of the current. If the water for some reason becomes particularly deep, as when floods sweep down the river, they may lose sight of landmarks in the turbulent muddy water and be carried downstream, unable to compensate for the current without their reference points. This may be part of the reason why young salmon come down the rivers when the water level rises, though this cannot be the complete explanation, for young salmon of different species vary in their behaviour at this time. Most, however, alter their behaviour quite strikingly and suddenly, from swimming up-stream and keeping station to going downstream seawards, at a particular time in their growth, probably under the influence of hormones. For they are active fish which need not be at the mercy of the current.

The migration of salmon is from fresh water to the sea and back again, perhaps to be repeated the next year. Fish which feed in the sea and breed in fresh water are called anadromous. Salmon do not feed on their journey up the river nor as they travel down again, so they arrive back at the sea lean and hungry. Yet they fed in the same river waters when they were young.

They spawn in the shallow head waters of the rivers and the young spend their early life there. At about two years, Atlantic salmon travel down the river and enter the sea. There they feed and grow, until at about four years they reach maturity and ascend the rivers to spawn, the spent fish dying in some species or, in others, returning to the sea in a very weakened condition to feed and reproduce again the following year. Sometimes fish ascend the rivers before their gonads are fully enlarged, early in the year long before the spawning season, forming a spring 'run,' while others do not swim up until later, close to the breeding season, when their gonads are well developed, the autumn 'run' (plate 11).

There is now a great deal of evidence, from the recapture of marked fish, that salmon tend to return to the river in which they spent their lives just before they went down to the sea. Errors are made but apparently only by a small proportion. An example of the results obtained is 469,326 king salmon marked, of which 2,492 were recovered in the lake in which they were released and 8,404 in parts of the river which were *en route* for the lake, and can be taken therefore as being on their way back. These figures at least show that many salmon do return to their home streams.

It would be of interest to know when their knowledge of the home stream is acquired, whether it is inherited, or learned. The test is to transfer salmon from the stream in which the eggs from which they were hatched were laid to other streams and observe their choice on return. The Lower Columbia river in British Colombia receives water from the Columbia river to the east and the Willamette to the south, both of which are fed by many tributaries. The king salmon—the Pacific coast salmon—

in the Columbia are autumn-run fish and those in the Willamette, spring run. Eggs were taken from redds, the spawning places, in the Willamette and hatched in the Columbia. The young fish were not set free until they were seven to eighteen months old and they were marked before their release. Four to five years later they were recaptured when they returned from the sea. They all came into the Columbia river where they were trapped. They were not so accurate at returning to the places from which they were liberated as fish which had lived there, but on the other hand the real inhabitants did not come up the Columbia until autumn, and the others came up in the spring when conditions for finding the right creek might not have been so good.

It seems then that the knowledge of the home—of whatever that knowledge may consist—is not inherited, though the making of spring or autumn runs apparently is, for it persists unchanged after the transfer. The fish learns to recognize its home during the early part of its life. Many animals—insects and birds, in particular—learn to recognize the place in which to lay their eggs, their parents, and the appearance of the opposite sex in the first moments of their existence outside the egg. Among birds it is often the experience of the first hours or days of life which determine much of their future behaviour. It might be that the young salmon also learns as firmly and as rigidly as a bird during its first hours, but there are indications that this firm knowledge of their home can be acquired later in life. Transfers of older fish show this. Yearling salmon will recognize the river to which they were transferred just as they are moving down river, but those which have to travel only 500 feet down their adopted stream are less accurate in finding it than those fish which have to swim a mile down it before reaching the main river. So the information can be learned at the age of one year but it apparently requires a little time.

How do they recognize the stream? The characteristics of each stream must remain constant throughout the fish's stay for three or four years in the sea. Further, the fish's memory of them must persist. A number of different suggestions have been made that the salmon reacts to carbon dioxide concentration, or to oxygen content, for example, but none of these is entirely satisfactory. It is clear that salmon are extremely sensitive to chemical substances. Many fish have very well developed olfactory senses. For example, a minnow is 250 times as sensitive as man to rose oil and 512 times as sensitive to cane sugar. Salmon, which were coming up a run, halted and even turned back downstream when a man dipped his hand, even for a short time, into the river above the run. In the laboratory it has been demonstrated that American blunt-nosed minnows can learn to distinguish between the water taken from two different streams, coming up for food when they perceive one kind of water and retreating when they sense the other. It seems that it is the dissolved organic substances which are active in determining the fishes' reaction, which is not surprising since most substances which have an odour are organic. Thus water coming from a watershed in which, owing to cultivation or the natural vegetation of the soil, may have organic constituents that differ from those in the soil in the drainage area of another stream. These experiments have not yet been carried out on salmon though a few salmon which had their nostrils plugged did not seem to choose the home stream so consistently but were scattered in the surrounding rivers almost at random, while those with their nostrils free found their home stream better.

There are a number of interesting points about the minnow-training experiments. Firstly, no matter at what season of the year the water samples were taken from the streams they were still distinguished by the minnows, which shows that the differences were constant, a feature which we have said is an essential. Secondly, the older minnows retained their memory of the differences for a shorter time than the younger ones. Now salmon learn the differences as young fish and might therefore, by analogy, be expected to retain the memory longer, as salmon are longer lived than minnows.

This may explain how they recognize their stream and, of

course, the river mouth out of which water from that stream, diluted many times with water from other tributaries, flows into the sea. Once recognized, the fishes' ability to perceive the direction of the current leads them upstream to the headwaters. But how do the fish return to the vicinity of the river mouth, when it is quite clear that they wander far away from its influence when they are in the sea? Once it seemed that the salmon remained within the area in which the river waters could be detected; they remained in fact where drift bottles set afloat near the river mouth moved. Since fresh water is lighter than salt the river water tends to float and not to mix immediately. But it is now quite clear that the salmon, both the Atlantic and Pacific kinds, travel great distances in the sea. For example, two Pacific pink salmon were marked as fry in Morrison Creek, a tributary of the Puntledge River, on Vancouver Island, B.C. Both were caught at sea in August and remarked. One of them was forty-five miles north of the creek, the other 115 miles south of it. In October both came on to the counting weir in their home stream. They must have returned by one of two ways. By one, they would have had to cross an area of sea in which water from another river, the Fraser—a large one with a big outflow—would be clearly recognizable; by the other they would have swum through tide flows where any gradient of chemical substances extending from their parent river would have been thoroughly confused by mixing, so preventing them from recognizing any specific river.

We may be able to suggest a way in which the salmon might perceive the correct river and go up it, but we have no idea how it navigates back to the river mouth. The concept of an inherited direction is no help as the fish still has to navigate in this direction and this is unexplained. Anyway, the two salmon just mentioned had turned in different directions on reaching the sea, which does not suggest an inherited direction, since we would expect it to be the same for all the fish from the same river, even if it were not essential. All we can say then is that, though the salmon may get away from the immediate influence of their 'own' river, they can still find their way back to it.

An even more remarkable return is that of eels which cover great distances to their rivers. These are surely some of the most remarkable animal journeys. As the result of the work of Johannes Schmidt in the 'twenties, we now know that the adult eels lay their eggs in the sea thousands of miles from the rivers in which they live. The story is perhaps well known now, but it is a sobering thought that the outline was only discovered thirty years ago and that only the outline is known even to-day. The mature eels, fat with deposits of reserve food, set off from the rivers of Europe, from the Baltic, the Mediterranean and from Britain to journey south-west or west to a point in the Sargasso Sea where, deep down, they spawn and die (fig. 58). On their journey to the breeding grounds they do not feed; indeed, their gut disappears. Other changes also take place in an eel's body. Their sense organs alter. Their eyes grow increasingly bigger until by the time the eels are well out to sea they have spread over most of the sides of their heads. No one can guess what these large eyes are for. They are not, apparently, for navigation for the eels usually move off on moonless nights. They cannot be for finding food, because the eels do not feed. The urge to migrate is apparently independent of the surroundings for when eels in rivers are active and beginning their migration, those in tanks also move about more than usual, rather like the migratory intention movements of caged wild birds (p. 107). The stimulus to migrate affects free and captive eels alike.

They swim on across the Atlantic, and are joined by eels from America swimming south-south-eastwards to reach a spawning area near that of the European eels. In the Sargasso Sea the water is warmer than off either continental coast and it is deep. On the other side of the world, the eels of the Dutch East Indies also seek deep warm water for their spawning, but they find it close to the coast. The eels never make the return journey; once the eggs have been laid, they die. Their young hatch as strange flat leptocephalus larvae (plate 12), so called

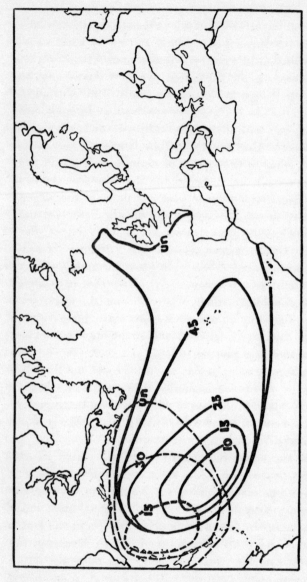

Fig. 58.—Spawning areas of eels in the Atlantic. The lines bound the areas in which leptocephali of the various lengths (in mms.) are found, *un* marks the boundary of the area beyond which no unmetamorphosed larvae are found. The broken lines represent the distribution of the American eel larvae and the full lines that of European eel larvae. (After Schmidt.)

because when they were first caught it was thought that they were a new sort of fish. They do not look like eels, and it was only later that their relationship to the long round eels of the rivers was realized. These are carried passively on the currents across the Atlantic to the coasts of Europe while the offspring of the American eels go northwards to the American seaboard. In the vicinity of the river mouths they turn into elvers which swim up the rivers in their thousands to change into adult eels.

The young may drift back to the rivers which are to form their homes for most of their adult life, but how do the mature fish find their way to the Sargasso Sea through thousands of miles of ocean apparently unrelieved by any landmarks? Even the explanation that like other spawning fish they swim against the current is a little hard to accept since the Gulf Stream, though a strong current on the west side of the Atlantic is very much weaker by the time it reaches the east side. There are no objects for the eels to steer by and it is difficult to see how they can perceive the current. Moreover, while they are coming down the rivers they are swimming with the current. It is possible that if they swim deep enough in the sea, they may get carried westwards by the current which travels in the opposite direction to the more superficial Gulf Stream.

There must be other signs by which they can navigate. They may perhaps be able to recognize the increasing temperature of the water. We know that some fish can detect temperature changes of between $0 \cdot 03°$ and $0 \cdot 1°$ C. Suppose that an eel is as sensitive as the most sensitive of these other fish, and that it can distinguish a temperature change of as little as $0 \cdot 03°$ C.; we still have no idea how quickly the change would have to be made for it to be detected. Would it have to be a very sudden drop or could it be a slow change, spread over a time? Let us, however, suppose that a temperature drop of $0 \cdot 03°$ C. can be sensed by an eel while swimming 100 metres, which is probably stretching our credulity anyway. Then if it started from the European coasts in water at $10°$ C., a reasonable temperature, after 100 kilometres at a change of $0 \cdot 03°$ C. every 100 metres it would be in a temperature of 40° C., in which in fact it would die. Thus it is very difficult to see how a sense of temperature change could carry the eels the distance they have to go without granting them a sensisitivity far beyond the bounds of anything conceivable. The same argument would apply if we supposed that they follow a gradient of increasing salinity. It has also been pointed out that if increased salinity and increased temperature were the clues, eels would not leave the Mediterranean, for off the Straits of Gibraltar the Atlantic has a lower salinity and a lower temperature than the water inside the Straits.

We are almost driven back to the idea of an inherited sense of direction, which we found that we had no reason to postulate for the return of salmon. We have seen that there are indications that birds may have an inborn sense, to judge, at least, from the stubbornness with which migrating birds maintain their direction when transported away from their route. Migrating adult eels in the Baltic maintain a direction between west-south-west and south-west, which if they persevered would lead them to the Sargasso Sea. But if they were heading for the geographical position of the Sea they would have to travel west-north-west. Furthermore, when silver eels caught off the Swedish coast were put down in a wet meadow they all wriggled away in one direction, so determinedly that when turned away from their course they turned back again as soon as possible. But the direction was not the same as they followed in the sea. If they really have such a sense of the direction in which they must swim it is most improbable that it is learned, for they leave the spawning area as eggs and drift, one supposes without exertion, as they journey to the coasts.

But it is a little hard to see how such a sense is used unless the inherited direction is a very general one—as indeed it probably is. For the young of eels which came from, say, Britain, may be carried to Spanish rivers. And there is apparently no certainty that an eel will return to the river, or even the country, from which its parents came. Yet the direction which an eel from North Britain must take to reach the Sargasso is rather

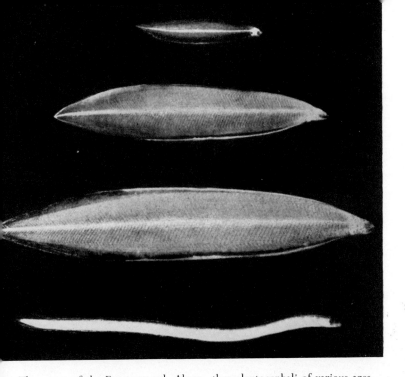

12 The young of the European eel. Above, three leptocephali of various ages and below, an elver

13 *Gymnarchus niloticus.* Note the waves travelling down the dorsal fin

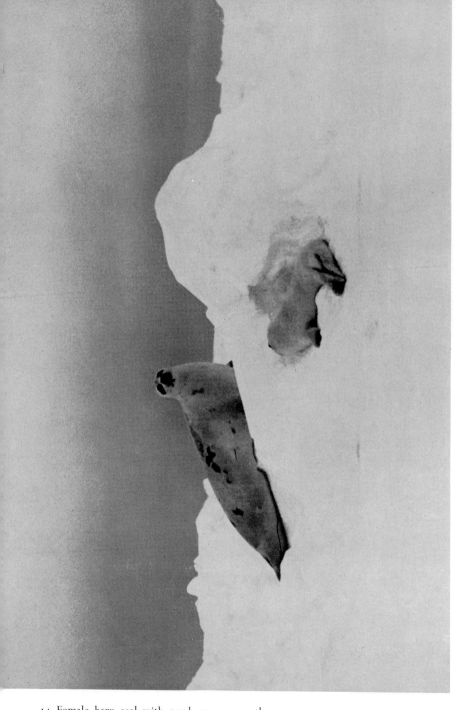

14 Female harp seal with newborn pup on the
breeding grounds off Labrador

different from that of a Spanish eel. But if the inherited direction has to be roughly westwards and the finer navigation to the Sargasso itself is done by detection of salinity and temperature changes nearer the destination, where the gradient is steeper, then this is more plausible.

It would be very interesting to know, but unfortunately impossible to discover, whether any strays come from the area where the American eels spawn and join the journey to Europe or whether their inherited tendency, which should lead them north, if anywhere, brings them back to their parents' home.

When we discussed bird navigation we could find little evidence that birds could detect the earth's magnetic field or electricity. Similarly it is most improbable that an electrical sense functions generally in fish or in sea fish, in particular. But though it has no bearing on the problem of migration it is interesting that several of the fish found in West African rivers and in the Nile generate their own electrical field and are sensitive to electricity. One of these, *Gymnarchus niloticus*, can swim equally well forwards and backwards (plate 13). When it is going backwards it apparently detects other fish in the muddy waters in which it lives because they cause disturbances in the field which it produces and which surrounds it. By this means it can navigate towards or away from them. Though fantastic and beyond our expectations, the existence of this sense should not lead us into extravagant theories of eels and salmon navigating by the earth's magnetic field. It is almost certainly unique to some groups of fishes and not found elsewhere. As a means of close-range location of prey it is obviously vitally important, but it is unlikely to function as a long-range navigational aid.

The mystery remains. This problem is going to be even harder to solve than bird navigation which, despite all the hard work, is only now showing the first signs of results.

CHAPTER IX

The Fated Journey

E VERY three or four years, thousands of small brown lemmings leave their usual mountain homes in southern Norway to come down into the plains and run towards the sea, and although usually nocturnal they now continue their journey by day. Each apparently knows the direction he must go, for they do not form bands unless some obstacle slows them down, as when they gather at the bank of a stream. When they reach the sea they plunge in, maintaining the direction they have been following and as they swim away they drown, having come to the end of that suicidal trek which has now become proverbial. The owls and other creatures which prey upon them enjoy an unexpected feast off the large numbers which suddenly appear, so to all the thousands which perish in the sea must be added the thousands which are picked off on their way.

Theirs is a one-way journey, for at the end lies death. Why they choose one direction and how they navigate we do not know. As for the reason why they set off, it seems that the population in their usual haunts builds up over the years to such a size that food supplies in the mountains are no longer sufficient. They burst out on to the lowlands to seek new food. Perhaps not all take part, for some must survive to found a new population.

But there are many mammals which move, like birds, between summer and winter quarters. They, too, often follow food supplies as they become available. In the early autumn the caribou that live on the Great Barrens region of Northern Canada move towards the timber line, and it was once thought they did so for shelter. They may start to move as early as July, usually heading southwards. But once among the timber they do not remain there, for in August or September they move a short distance north again, only to turn south once more to spend the rest of the winter wandering in the forests of Alberta, Saskatchewan and Manitoba. In all probability their migrations are a search for food, for deep snow makes it very difficult or impossible for the caribou to reach the lichens upon which they feed. This may be the reason why in other parts of their range, they move away from the exposed sides of mountains where the snow gathers, to congregate on the sheltered side. Their young are born during the spring migration and the herds have no definite breeding ground.

On the other hand there are some aquatic mammals that make long journeys to very circumscribed breeding places. Harp seal breeding grounds, for example, are in three main areas, off Labrador, between Iceland and Spitzbergen, and in the White Sea. They come out on the ice to have their pups, which stay there until they are old enough to swim (plate 14). In the White Sea the pups are carried northwards by the movement of the pack ice as it breaks away in the spring. When they are old enough they swim actively, spreading farther north, for marked seals from the White Sea have been recaptured off Nova Zemlja, and even, eight years after marking, off Spitzbergen.

The Pribilof Islands are the scene of the yearly gathering of Alaskan fur seals. Here the young are born and when they can they leave with their mothers to swim some 3,000 miles south to the warmer waters off the coasts of Southern California. The males, however, do not go far; they remain in the waters around the Aleutian Islands, rejoining their mates on the Pribilofs the following year.

Whales also migrate. Though there are many details to be filled in, it is becoming clear that many species, hunted in the Antarctic, breed in the warmer waters nearer the equator and later move south to feed and grow. Sperm whales probably breed as far north as the Azores-Madeira area, while humpbacked whales marked in the Antarctic have been found off north-west Australia and Madagascar (fig. 59). It is striking to see how close whales are found in subsequent years to the place where they were originally marked though meanwhile they must have migrated north and returned at least once.

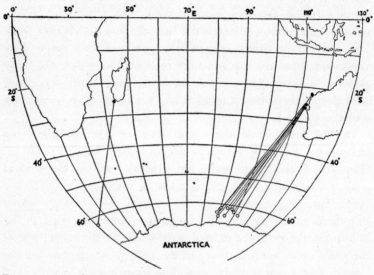

Fig. 59.—Map showing distribution of fin whales marked in the Antarctic (o) in the southern summer and captured (●) about eighteen months later. (After Rayner.)

We have no idea what guides the herds of caribou, whales or seals on their journeys. None of them are animals which lend themselves to homing experiments. But the smaller mammals, like wild mice, are easily captured and transported, and experiments have been carried out which involved observing their return from some distance away from the area in which they have been captured. White-footed mice of various species live in the forests of North America. In general they do not roam far; males probably run 150 feet at the most, while females travel less. We know this because mice trapped alive, marked and released, are rarely recaptured outside these limits. Yet if they are taken very much farther away they may still return to their home area. In one set of experiments, out of forty-nine animals, five returned from 1 mile away and one from 1½ miles. Only one mouse out of twenty-three returned from 2 miles, and none of the fifteen mice released 4 miles away were recaptured in their

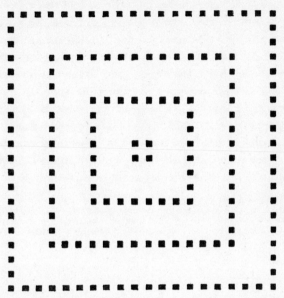

FIG. 60.—Arrangement of trapping boxes in experiment on wild mouse homing. (After Stickel.)

original area. The limit beyond which they were unable to find their homes was clear.

Another more elaborate series of experiments was done in a section of woodland in the Patuxent Research Refuge in Maryland. The locality was chosen because it did not seem to a human to contain any obvious landmarks and was surrounded on all sides by more woodland, so that any mice in the section could not see landmarks outside its boundaries. Traps were put down in three concentric squares, each trap being 55 feet away from its neighbour in the row, while the squares were 165 feet apart. There were four traps in the centre (fig. 60). The whole arrangement covered 22·5 acres.

For the first two days mice were marked and released where

they were caught. On the third day, however, all the mice found in the outer traps were released at the centre of the squares. Then no trapping was done for five days; this allowed any mice which were journeying back to find their way without being interrupted. And many of them did find their way back, for when trapping was resumed and carried on for three days, seventeen males and ten females were found in the same traps from which they had come, while most of the remainder were in traps close to their old ones. At the same time, to make sure that something was not causing all the mice to start moving about, trapping on the other two squares was continued, though these animals had not been transferred. None of the outer square animals were found in these traps, and the animals caught were very faithful to their own areas as the results showed:

Shortest distance between the traps in which the mice were first found and those in which they were recaptured.	Animals transferred (i.e. from outer squares.)		Animals not transferred.	
	Males	Females	Males	Females
0	17	10	11	14
55	5	3	4	4
110	1	0	1	1
165	1	1	0	0
173	0	0	2	0
595	0	1	0	0
765	1	0	0	0
Not recaptured	2	6	2	0
	27	21	20	19

so these small animals were able to home over distances between 500 and 700 feet, considerably greater than their normal range of 100 to 150 feet.

We can only conjecture how the mice found their way. It seems most improbable that the ones from the outer squares knew the centre of the area, when we consider that if a mouse is to be able to home from any direction over a distance three times its normal range, that is 450 feet for a male, it must have knowledge of landmarks over an area nine times its normal range. When we remember that in the first experiment mice returned from distances more than ten times their usual wandering distance we see how huge an area we should have to suppose the mice to know. Add to all this the fact that the mice which returned from $1\frac{1}{2}$ and 2 miles were immature animals between four and eight weeks old, which we would not expect to know areas as far away as this, and we see even more forcibly that it is most unlikely that the mice were necessarily returning over ground with which they were familiar. Those that came back from 100 to 200 feet had doubtless already been where they were released. But as regards those mice which covered the greater distances, there seems no alternative but to say that they used some method which did not depend upon known landmarks. This does not exclude sun navigation of some sort, but neither for this nor for any other method have we positive evidence, nor have any experiments been devised to test the existence of a navigational aid.

The time the mice take seems to vary. The bank voles of the Austrian forests were used for another set of experiments so arranged that the time they took to reach home could be recorded. There seemed to be no connection between the distance they had to cover and how long they took. If anything it seemed that as the animals grew older their ability to home from greater distances increased. Animals less than two months old did not return, even from 250 metres, yet those of nine months or more than a year old returned from 300 metres in 10 to 15 minutes. This suggests that the range which the animal knows increases as it grows older and presumably explores farther and farther afield. But this increase in range seems to be irregular, extending farther in one direction than in others. Voles which had returned successfully from a given distance in one direction could not do so from the same distance in another direction. As to the landmarks they used, we can only suppose that those which the mice learned where probably near the ground or on it, for the forests were thick on the slopes leading down to a lake where the experiments were done and might exclude a continuous view of more distant landmarks and perhaps of the sun and sky themselves.

These small mammals, easily trapped and transported, lend themselves to homing experiments, though from all this work nothing definite has emerged. But we are all familiar with the stories of the return of various household pets to their old homes after moving house with their owners. Cats are so prone to this that a great variety of ways of making them stay at their new home have been prescribed and embedded in folk-lore. A sovereign but expensive cure for a cat's wanderlust is said to be buttering their paws. But cats are individualists:

> They slip, diminished neat, through loopholes
> Less than themselves; will not be pinned
> To rules or routes for journeys . . . .

So newspapers will continue to have items like the following, despite all the efforts of mere humans to curb their cats' propensities.

CAT WALK. Snooky, a ginger tom cat, has just completed a journey on foot of 135 miles, from his new home at Gloucester, to his old home at Balsham, near Cambridge. It took him 22 days.

Dogs, too, will follow their masters for long distances. And horses' abilities to remember a route are said to have saved many a wounded cavalryman on the field of battle and have even been used in crime detection. During the war, near Marburg, in Germany, a thief stole some goods from a shop. He loaded his loot on a cart in a nearby farm, harnessed up the farmer's horse and drove off. The horse and cart were found later abandoned in Marburg. The farmer took his horse back, reharnessed it to the empty cart and allowed the horse to wander off without a restraining hand on the reins, but closely followed by farmer and police. It followed the road, until it turned off across some fields and round the edge of some woods to an old bunker in which was found the loot the thief had hidden there before abandoning the horse in the streets of the town. This is only one of the many stories which show that a horse has an excellent memory of the route it has covered.

But this time we can go further and say at least something

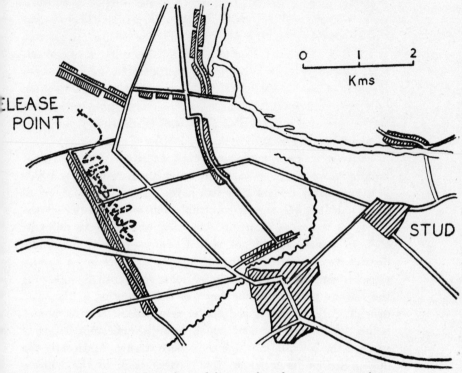

Fig. 61.—A horse taken from the stud farm to the release point × without seeing the surroundings followed the broken line before being recaptured. (After Grzimek.)

about what a horse uses to recognize a route. As might be expected of an animal with such well-developed vision but such a poorly developed sense of smell, it seems to recognize landmarks visually. Five Arab mares were blindfolded and either transported or led distances of between $5\frac{1}{2}$ and 15 kilometres. Then, with the blindfolds removed, they were left to their own devices. None of them were able to return home but wandered about apparently aimlessly (fig. 61).

Tales of animals that have found their way home over long distances have to be examined critically, for it is not always certain that they have not been over the country before. For example, there is the tale of a cavalry horse which was taken by train from the military stables in Potsdam to Hirschberg, some 250 kilometres away. It broke away and was back in its old stall at Potsdam in five days. Superficially this looks like a remarkable feat, but there does seem to be considerable doubt whether Hirschberg was completely new country. If it was not then the horse was relying on its memory, a remarkable thing in itself but not so shrouded in the blinding mists of extra-sensory powers as it might have seemed.

Fortunately, on a number of occasions people have tested the homing powers of dogs by transporting them to districts which it is reasonably certain they had never visited before. Some of their journeys are almost incredible but the authority of the observers is beyond question. One dog was taken 20 miles by train to a place it had not visited before—in fact, the whole district was unfamiliar to it as its master was spending a holiday there. It returned to its temporary home apparently by following the railway track. Another dog was taken hunting in the same district. Afterwards dog and master returned to their temporary home, travelling by a boat which made several stops before it reached the town near which they were staying. Apparently the dog preferred its freedom, for it went back to the hunting grounds, travelling by the same boat service and remaining on board until it came to the correct landing place. The dog did this journey several times and was seen by a member of the crew to board the boat unaided and to leave it unprompted by anybody.

From the example of the horse it is tempting to say that visual landmarks are most important in dog homing. Unfortunately there are few cases in which the routes that the dogs took are known and no records of experiments with blindfolded dogs. In two cases, both from Germany, we do have the details, however (plates 15 and 16). Maxl, a mongrel Scottish sheepdog, which

lived in the country was taken by his master to a place 6 kilometres away by a roundabout route. It is fairly safe to assume for
various reasons that he had never been to this place, and from it
he could not see his home, for there were hills in between. He
was released in the morning. For half an hour he walked about in
no particular direction, without leaving the area where he found
himself. The dog looked excited, according to those watching
him; he panted, though he was not exerting himself and the day
was not hot. Then he started off in the direction of home without
much hesitation about the direction. He arrived back home one
hour and eight minutes later. Eighteen days after, the test was
repeated, this time he set off after only six minutes' delay and
arrived back in forty-three minutes. The route he followed was
a more direct one than on the first occasion. On yet a third
occasion he wandered away in the early part of his journey, but
followed a more direct path during the latter part (plate 15).

A bitch, Nora, belonging to the same master, was a town
dweller. She was let loose in a part of Munich which it is improbable that she knew. Once again, a period of indecision
preceded the dog's setting off homewards. She maintained her
direction, though she stopped to play with other dogs on the
way. It took her two hours and ten minutes to get home, in
which time she travelled 8·5 kilometres (plate 16). Forty days
later she was released in the same place, and turned homewards.
But this time she followed a different, shorter route (5 kilometres) and reached home in thirty-five minutes. Both these
journeys were made in the early morning, when the streets were
empty.

Neither of these dogs had apparently learned a fixed route
once they had managed to get home the first time. They seemed
to know a series of general directions in which to travel. It does
not look therefore as if they remembered the details of houses
or road surfaces, for if they had we would expect them to follow
their first route exactly when they returned on subsequent
occasions. The fact that they clearly did not might be interpreted as being due to their following some overall visual land-

mark such as the sun's direction rather than the details of their immediate surroundings. But we have no evidence that, like the horses, these dogs were using their eyes to home. Dogs have such

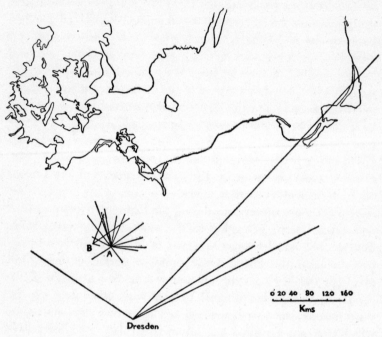

Fig. 62.—Some of the results obtained when bats were transported from caves in the Brandenburg area (A and B), and from Dresden. (After Eisentraut.)

a well-developed sense of smell that it is certainly possible that they may have been following scent landmarks. We can say nothing more.

Resemblances between bats and birds stimulated some experiments on homing with these flying mammals. The results have shown not only that bats can home from unknown areas but that like birds they too migrate seasonally. Dr. Eisentraut marked 8,295 mouse-eared bats in Brandenburg over a period of ten years. Recovery rates of marked bats were about equal to those of song birds, for Dr. Eisentraut managed to awake the enthusiasm of many naturalists on the Continent, who then formed his corps of watchers. Thus out of all of the mouse-eared bats he marked, 199 were recovered. The places in which

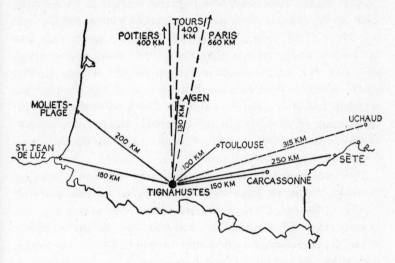

Fig. 63.—Some places to which bats from the grotto of Tignahustes were transported and released. The solid lines indicate successful return, while a broken line indicates that at the time the experiment was reported no bats had returned. (After Casteret.)

they were found showed that the Brandenburg caves were their winter shelters though they spent the summer on the average between 20 and 50 miles away, in directions between north-west and south-east of the city (fig. 62). They returned most accurately to their winter quarters, the same bats being found in the same caves and even in the same places within the cave, year after year. Noctule bats make longer journeys apparently, one of those banded in Dresden was recovered in the summer 470 miles away in Lithuania.

The famous French cave explorer, Norbert Casteret, studied the mouse-eared bats in some of the Pyrénéan caves. He noticed that they arrived at about the same time as the swallows in the spring and left in August. Again, the marked bats remained faithful to the caves they had already inhabited. He took bats away to release them and found that they could return from areas which had large numbers of caves, which did not seem to confuse them. Two hundred kilometres seemed to be near the limit of the distance from which they could return, for they did not home from Tours, Poitiers or Paris, all more than 400 kilometres away, though they came back from nearer places (fig. 63). But on release near Paris a bat did at once fly due south, which is the direction of the grotto of Tignahustes from which it had come. But it is also the direction of the city with its promise of roosting places, so perhaps the bat was concentrating more on its immediate needs than on distant possibilities in the Pyrénées.

Bats are essentially nocturnal creatures. Casteret's bats, for example, began to leave their roosts 20 to 30 minutes after sundown, the caves being evacuated in one hour to one hour and a half. They all returned by half-past two in the morning. Probably, therefore, they flew only by night on their way home. This rules out any form of sun navigation.

The situation is rather similar to that of locust navigation, for we know little of the methods of long range migration among bats, but we know quite a lot about their short range navigation. Bats are remarkable for their ability to avoid obstacles in the dark—or light, for that matter. They do not get themselves entangled in the hair of every girl in the vicinity, as custom assumes. Some people can hear bats squeaking, but the squeak is out of the range of most peoples' hearing, especially older people. In fact analysis reveals that the noises bats make can be divided into three, an audible cry at a frequency of about 7,000 cycles, a supersonic cry which is loudest at 45,000 to 55,000 cycles per second, and an audible click. The highest note of a piano has a frequency of 4,224 cycles per second and the average upper limit of perception by the human ear is about 15,000 cycles per second, so the supersonic cry is well outside the range of human hearing. But it is this cry which is responsible for the bat's ability to locate obstacles. High frequency waves of this sort are reflected from objects, and more quickly, of course, from nearer than from more distant ones.

Bats are entirely dependent on this echolocation at night, for blindfolded bats can avoid a row of fine wires hung in a room but they can do so no longer if their ears are covered or their mouths are closed. In the first case they can no longer hear the reflected sound and in the second they can no longer make it. Bats can perform amazing feats of avoiding obstacles using this method. A barrier of wires, 1 mm. in diameter, hung at 30 cm. intervals across a room is hit by some bats on only seven occasions in one hundred flights through the barrier.

The design of the mechanism is quite beautiful. For example, if the bat could hear its own squeaks as it made them it would be unable to hear the echo. But when a bat squeaks—and it does so in bursts lasting about two-and-a-half thousandths of a second —a small muscle puts its ear mechanism temporarily out of order, so that its ear is fully efficient immediately afterwards. Of course a bat's vocal membranes are specially adapted to produce high frequency sound, being thin and very tightly stretched. Thus several parts of the head are specialized for echo location.

Echolocation had been used by humans long before the invention of more scientific methods of sounding. In a fog, ships' captains would sound their sirens and could tell from the echoes how far from the shore they were. Some sailors declared that they could by this means detect even comparatively small objects like buoys. The senses of blind people are often sharpened beyond the normal. A blind man's stick serves not only to feel objects but also to set up sound waves the echoes of which can tell a great deal to one who is sensitive to them. Some blind people volunteered for a test in which their ears were covered; they could not then guide themselves. There are blind people who even disdain the help of a stick for they can find their way by the echoes of their footsteps. Finally, a radar device based on the principle of bat's echolocation has been devised, small enough to be carried comfortably by a blind person.

We have dismissed the idea that animals have a 'sense of

direction,' but it is often claimed that some men have a 'bump of direction.' It seems that some tribes, especially those that live in the desert, have the ability to tell the direction in which they should set off across a featureless landscape. To this day Arab navigators, sailing from Africa to India, often reject navigational aids. But there is no need to assume a 'sixth sense,' for there are many natural indications of direction if one is sufficiently aware of them and able to interpret them. The sun is the most obvious, and in the desert the direction of the run of sand dunes is determined by the prevailing wind. People who live close to the land get to know these natural signposts, though they may not always understand the reasons behind them. Often the use of this sort of knowledge is unconscious and so appears to be a 'sixth sense.' But in reality we need not extend the sensory powers of human beings beyond those we are more accustomed to consider.

We look at animals wandering over the earth and wonder at their powers of navigation but our wonder is really a measure of our lack of knowledge of the workings of animals' senses. Nevertheless though so many different mammals habitually navigate on land, in the sea and in the air, we know remarkably little about how they do it, closely related though they are to ourselves.

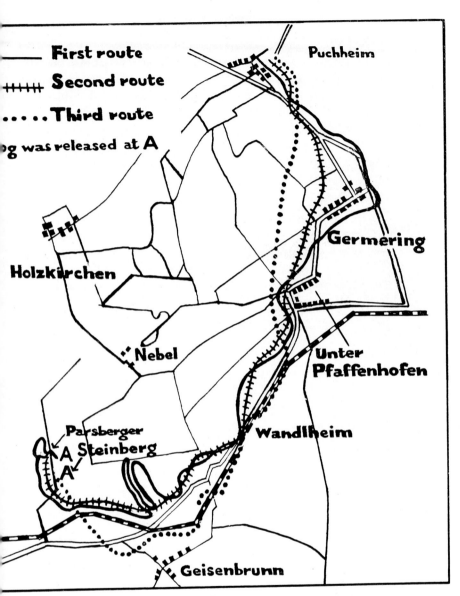

15 The tracks of the dog 'Maxl' after he had been
transported from Puchheim and released at A.
(From Schmid)

16 The tracks of the bitch 'Nora' as sh
returned home (E) from place A
Munich. After following the track A₁—
on her first return, she was carried to ʌ
and released, when she ran home alon
A₂—E₂. On her second return from
she ran along A—E. (From Schmid)

CHAPTER X

Animal Senses

⚔

THE evidence that animals are not scattered like leaves in the wind but can go where they wish or where their innate tendencies lead them is overwhelming. Death through being cast on stony ground is not for them unless something goes amiss with their behavioural responses. But there are flaws in this façade of efficiency; the mass drowning of lemmings, leading to their destruction by their inherited responses, is not unique. Locusts, for example, also perform 'mad migrations,' occasionally flying out to sea when they reach the coast. But in view of the extraordinary senses postulated for animals to explain their most striking navigational abilities, it would be worthwhile to conclude by reviewing those which we know are used.

It is evident that no new senses have yet been proved to exist, and in particular, sensitivity to the earth's magnetic field has not been demonstrated. Some fish are sensitive to alterations in the electrical field they set up, but apart from this exceptional electrical sensitivity we have not had need to fall back on this unproven sense. We have been able to suggest explanations for most animals' navigational ability by their sensitivity to light, chemicals, touch or sound.

Animals may be much more sensitive to these stimuli than we are. This is demonstrated by a fish's ability to detect tiny concentrations of chemicals in the water, but the basic mechanism of the sense organs probably remains the same as our own. Insects are particularly sensitive to chemicals—though the structure of their sense organs is different from ours. Of this the most striking instance is the way in which male moths from miles away will gather round a captive female or even round a box in which she has been. The attenuation of her body scent over such distances must be very great indeed and the males must be sensitive to very low concentrations of chemical.

However, different aspects of stimulation familiar to us may be apparent to animals. Tastes have shapes to ants, for example. But the most striking of these differences is the ability of insects to detect the polarization of light. At one time it seemed necessary to suppose that ants could see the stars by day, there seemed no other way in which they could navigate—as they were seen to do—without landmarks and with the sun hidden from them. We can now discard this rather weird theory and show that they can see the pattern of polarized light in the sky, for the structure of an individual part, an ommatidium, of their compound eye makes this possible. Each contains a potential analyser of the light. As the ommatidia are packed together pointing radially outwards, the whole eye covers a large field of the surroundings, sometimes as much as 180 deg. in the horizontal plane, so that objects directly in front and directly behind are seen (plate 17). But the ommatidia are to a large extent independent of each other. This makes the whole eye a more efficient instrument for this sort of navigation than is the eye of a vertebrate. The existence of a number of units means that insects can move until a particular pattern of light is received by one, or by a group, of these units and then modify its future behaviour to keep the pattern in that unit. This would be a more difficult, if not impossible, task in an eye with a retina composed of cells which are not screened from each other, and which are more closely linked together by nerves than the ommatidia for the retina is not partitioned in the same way as the total light sensitive screen of an insect is. Under these conditions it seems that it would be impossible to localize the pattern with any great accuracy.

The same argument applies to the superiority of the compound eye as the receptor in a light compass reaction. If the animal is to move at a constant angle to a beam of light, for

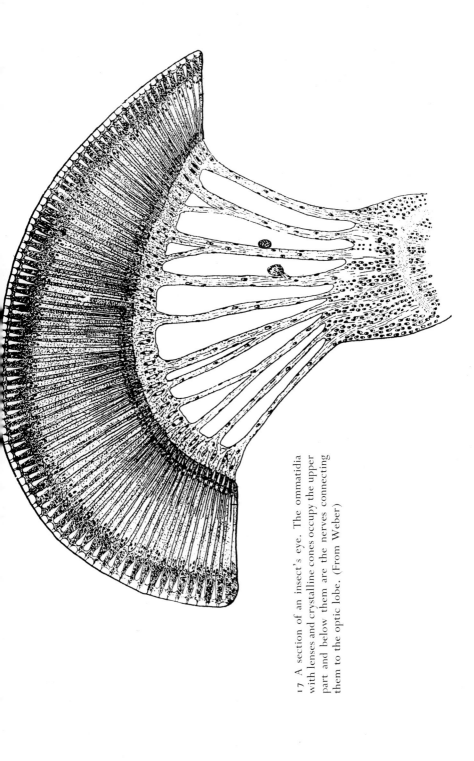

17 A section of an insect's eye. The ommatidia with lenses and crystalline cones occupy the upper part and below them are the nerves connecting them to the optic lobe. (From Weber)

18 Guacháros, from Brehm's *Illustriertes Tierleben* (1891)

example, the light can be maintained in one ommatidium. We can only perform this sort of navigation crudely, for though we may walk 'keeping the sun on our right hand,' we get only a general direction in this way; we cannot estimate accurately where to go.

This is also because on a long journey we rarely make allowances for the sun's movement. But navigators, using the sun, must do so, and accuracy in navigation depends upon the accuracy of the chronometer used. It is not surprising therefore to find that a time sense is well developed in many of those animals which use the sun for navigation. Birds have an internal 'clock' which enables them to learn to go to a particular box for food, marking it by its relationship to the sun's direction, but allowing for the fact that this relationship alters during the day. Again, sandhoppers were kept in a room with successive twelve hours of darkness and twelve of light arranged twelve hours out of phase with the day/night cycle outside. After this treatment they navigated inaccurately, their average mistake being very close to the 180 deg. angle between correct and incorrect direction which might be expected, since their 'day' was out of phase by half a cycle (fig. 64).

Bees can allow for the movement of the polarized light pattern. They have a well-developed time sense which they display when they learn to visit a feeding place only at one definite time of day. For a nectar gatherer, such a time sense is important, since it enables the animal to use its foraging efforts economically, for some flowers do not yield nectar throughout the day but only at particular times. The bees apparently learn to recognize these times, for they do not visit those flowers except at the appropriate hour. When they are given drugs which increase the speed of their metabolism they arrive early, and when they are cooled, which retards their bodily processes, they are late. So their time sense depends upon internal processes, for external 'time' does not immediately cause any change, though rhythmic changes of temperature or light, for example, may modify the internal rhythm after a time. Bees were transported between feeds from the Continent to New York where they were put into a room exactly like their European one; they emerged to find their food at the same time as

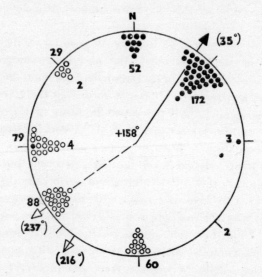

Fig. 64.—Sandhoppers which had been kept in artificial 'day/night' conditions twelve hours out of step with the real day/night (●) moved in a different direction to hoppers which had not been subjected to this treatment (○). The actual heading of the shortest distance to the sea was 216 deg. The figures within the circle represent the numbers of experimental animals and those outside the control animals, each ○ or ● being equivalent to 5 observations. (After Pardi and Grassi.)

their home time, ignoring the fact that time in New York was five or six hours behind that at home and the sun outside—which they could not see—had not moved as far across the sky as would have been the case at home.

It often occurs in the animal kingdom that a mechanism which allows one animal to perform some particular part of its activities is also found in another quite unrelated animal. Bat echolocation is a good example of this, for it is now known that a similar method of obstacle location is used by cave-dwelling birds, the guacháros of Venezuela (plate 18). These are large birds, measuring three-and-a-half feet from wing-tip to wing-tip. Though they nest in caves and spend their days there, they come out at night to feed on fruit. Professor Griffin, of Harvard University, found that within the caves—where they live in utter darkness—they fly about making a great deal of noise, but as they leave the caves in the twilight they are quieter, making only audible clicks. When he recorded these and analysed them he found that they are bursts of sound lasting one to two thousandths of a second. In duration, therefore, they are very like the exploratory sounds made by bats, though their frequency, 7,000 cycles a second, is lower, so that the bird's click is plainly audible to us while the bat's is not. In a darkened room, these birds, with their ears plugged, flew into the walls which they were able to avoid in the light. However, when the ear plugs were removed they were able to avoid hitting the walls even in darkness. Professor Griffin has pointed out that the accuracy of this navigational aid is less than that of a bat owing to the longer wavelength of the sound that the bird utters. The shorter the wavelength the smaller the object which can be detected, so the bird cannot locate obstacles as small as can the bat.

There seems, ultimately, no reason why all animal navigation should not be explained in terms of sensitivity to sources of stimuli familiar to man. A difficulty which must be overcome in thinking about this problem lies in our desire, conscious or unconscious, to parallel animals' senses with our own. But willingness to admit the possibility of the superiority of animals' senses in some directions should not lead us into the realms of fantasy, where so many have wandered while considering the remarkable powers of animals to navigate.

INDEX

GEORGE ALLEN & UNWIN LTD
London: 40 Museum Street, W.C.1

Auckland: 24 Wyndham Street
Bombay: 15 Graham Road, Ballard Estate, Bombay 1
Calcutta: 17 Chittaranjan Avenue, Calcutta 13
Cape Town: 109 Long Street
Karachi: Haroon Chambers, South Napier Road, Karachi 2
New Delhi: 13–14 Ajmeri Gate Extension, New Delhi 1
São Paulo: Avenida 9 de Julho 1138–Ap. 51
Sydney, N.S.W.: Bradbury House, 55 York Street
Toronto: 91 Wellington Street West